SEEING • ORGANIZING • ACTING • REJECTING

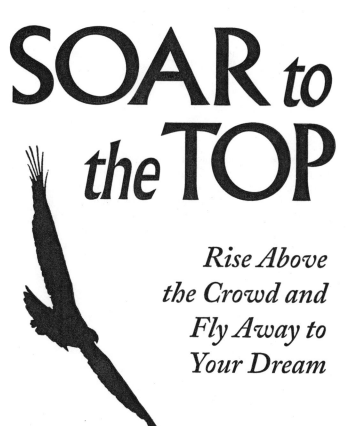

SOAR to the TOP

*Rise Above
the Crowd and
Fly Away to
Your Dream*

SHAWN ANDERSON

SOAR TO THE TOP

SHAWN ANDERSON
Copyright©2001 by Shawn Anderson
ISBN 0-938716-41-7

Published by
POSSIBILITY PRESS
e-mail: PossPress@excite.com

Cover photo: Digital Imagery© copyright 2001 PhotoDisc, Inc.

Manufactured in the United States of America

Other Books by *Possibility Press*

Tapes by *Possibility Press*

DEDICATION

To Christine...it is your model of consistency and excellence that I seek to duplicate. You gracefully *SOAR* through life with amazing brilliance.

ACKNOWLEDGMENTS

To Joe—thank you for your effort on this project and for your extraordinary talent which has motivated me greatly. I will always be grateful for your lifelong friendship, which started in the first grade.

A special tribute to Og Mandino, Dale Carnegie, and other success speakers and authors who have influenced me over the years. It was your dedication to sharing the message of hope and personal empowerment that changed the way I view life. You were the ones who planted the seeds of this book a long time ago.

Also, a sincere thank you to the staff at Possibility Press for your belief in me and my message, as well as your patience, time, effort, and creativity in helping make this book what it has become.

CONTENTS

"'Come to the cliff,' he said. They said, 'We are afraid.' 'Come to the cliff,' he said. They came. He pushed them. And they flew."

—Stuart Wilde

FOREWORD

I have a great deal of respect and admiration for Shawn and his desire to empower others to maximize their potential. He has an infectious enthusiasm for excellence that I find incredibly motivating.

Secondly, I believe in Shawn's words. Whether it's in your business or personal life, this book can help you produce dynamic results. He's done a fantastic job of melting the success principles into a powerful four-step formula...Seeing, Organizing, Acting, and Rejecting. I wholeheartedly believe that, in these four steps, you will not only find the secrets that life's all-star achievers have known, but you will also multiply your own ability to grow and become the person you want to be, and live the life you want to live.

SOAR To The Top! is all about how to make your dream and goals come true. It's about helping you identify your purpose, develop life passion, and achieve personal mastery. I am pleased to attach my name to a product that can help people bring those elements into their lives.

I hope you let the amazing concept of *SOAR To The Top!* touch your mind and inspire your heart. With this tool, you will never look the same way again at obstacles that threaten to impede you on your path of success. Put *SOAR To The Top!* into action and you can produce life-changing results.

One more note about Shawn...he writes from his heart. He stirs your emotions, giving your intellect time to kick in so you can see that his approach will work in real life. Watch Shawn Anderson. He is an excellent communicator who has the ability to touch lives. God has enormous plans for him, and you will undoubtedly reap the rich overflow of his life.

Jim Gibbons, Member, United States Congress

Webster's Dictionary says...

To Soar / so(e)r /, v.

1. Is to rise, fly, or glide high and apparently with little effort.

2. Is to climb swiftly or powerfully.

3. Is to rise or aspire to a...higher level.

Or, you could say...

To Soar / so(e)r /, v.

1. Is to push myself past my precon-
ceived and self-imposed limitations
so I can achieve my goals and live
my dream.

2. Is to live a life of new possibilities
—confronting and conquering even
the greatest of my personal and
business challenges.

3. Is to believe that I *can* accomplish
anything I set my mind to do. *I
can make it happen!*

"Once you have tasted flight, you will walk the earth with your eyes turned skyward, for there you have been, and there you long to return."

—*Leonardo da Vinci*

AUTHOR'S DARE...

*"What kind of man would live where there is no daring?
I don't believe in taking foolish chances, but nothing
can be accomplished without taking any chance at all."*
Charles Lindbergh

Have you ever watched a lone eagle flying gracefully over the wide-open spaces, *soaring* high above it all? It seems oblivious to the danger below and unafraid to climb to breathtaking heights.

What a feeling of power the eagle must have, knowing he has complete freedom to climb without limits—to *soar* over breathtaking landscapes to destinations of his choice. He is truly the master of his domain.

Think of how exciting it would be to have that same uninhibited freedom to *soar* in your own life! Imagine having the confidence to fully extend yourself, to reach for your goals and dreams. Imagine *soaring* to dizzying heights others are afraid to seek because of their fear of failing.

By learning how to *SOAR,* you can unleash yourself from self-imposed limitations. You can accomplish your ambitions, which you may have thought of as mere fantasy. They were only wishes you believed might come true *someday,* which is simply another word for never. Knowing how to *SOAR* can lead you to a more satisfying personal life, as well as giving you wings to reach new heights in your career or business.

In *SOAR To The Top,* you'll find the proven truths of how to succeed and make a difference in a memorable way. This book also holds the secret to igniting your passion. By giving you the keys to live a more empowered and self-directed life, *SOAR To The Top* will guide you in "rising above the crowd."

When you learn to *SOAR* you can accomplish whatever you choose to. Go ahead and do it. I dare you to take off and *SOAR!*

Introduction

The Art of *SOARING* . . .

*"You can never consent to creep
when you feel the impulse to soar."*
Helen Keller

You Have the Freedom to *SOAR*

Soaring in life is easier than most people will lead you to believe. In fact, the word itself gives you all the clues you need.

The letters that make up the acronym *SOAR* represent principles that, when applied to your life, empower you with the ability to fly your own course. Follow the principles rooted in these four letters. Uncover the potential that might otherwise have remained shrouded beneath veils of self-doubt and regret. Start working toward living the life you've always dreamed about.

The S Stands for *SEEING*—

SEEING yourself succeeding and accomplishing great goals and dreams. *SEEING* is picturing the future...your future!

The O Stands for *ORGANIZING*—

ORGANIZING your goals and dreams and developing a specific plan of action so you can achieve them. *ORGANIZING* is understanding and thinking about the steps that will allow you to be successful in your mission.

The A Stands for *ACTING*—

ACTING on your plans and goals—being a *DO IT NOW* person! *ACTING* is motivating yourself and doing whatever it takes to make it happen.

"What you end up becoming you become by effort."

The R Stands for *REJECTING*—
REJECTING failures and defeatist attitudes that can cause you to quit before you achieve your goal. *REJECTING* is having the determination and perseverance to overcome the obstacles that temporarily impede your success.

SEEING—ORGANIZING—ACTING—REJECTING

This book introduces you to these four cornerstones of success and explains how you can master each one in pursuit of your dream. By incorporating each principle into your life you develop mastery over it! It's that simple...

Now SOAR to the top, onward and upward!

High Flight

*Oh, I have
slipped the surly bonds of
earth and danced the skies on
laughter's silver wings. Sunward I
have climbed and joined the
tumbling mirth of sun-split clouds,
and done a hundred things you have
not dreamed of. Wheeled and soared
and swung high in the sunlit silence.
Hovering there, I have chased the
shouting wind alone and flown my
eagle craft through footless halls of
air. Up, up the long, delirious
burning blue, I have topped the
wind-swept heights with easy grace
where never lark or even eagle flew.
And then, with silent lifting mind, I
have trod the high, untrespassed
sanctity of faith, put out my hand,
and touched the face of God.*

—John Gillespie Magee, Jr.

Chapter 1

UNLOCKING YOUR POTENTIAL TO *SOAR*— THE BLUEPRINT TO BUILDING YOUR DREAMS

"Nothing happens unless first a dream."
Carl Sandburg

Make a Decision—*Then Take Action*

Reading this book clearly shows you have a desire to make the most of your life. This bold decision separates you from those who only wish they had a better life, but never take action to make it happen. No matter where you are on your journey, take satisfaction knowing you are *now taking action*.

The *SOAR* approach to success is simple. Successful living isn't rocket science—it's done by ordinary people who dedicate themselves to getting extraordinary results. But, how can you do it too? Believe in yourself and your dreams, and live with passion. Follow the simple success principles represented by *SOAR*, and make your dreams come true.

Succeed and fulfill your dreams by following the four principles highlighted by the simple acronym *SOAR*. How successful can you be? As much as you want and believe you can be! For example, if you want to build a big business or a great career, you can do it. You make the decision—*you build the dream!* When you reach one dream, build a bigger one. The *SOAR* approach is simply a set of blueprints to move on.

Throughout this book, you'll be given questions to ask yourself to help you widen your horizons so you can think bigger and get in touch with your true potential. Rather than just reading over these questions, stop and give them some thought. Your answers will give you the clues you need to benefit from the possibilities that lie ahead for you. Feel free to continue your answers on an additional sheet of paper if you need more space. Now, let's start *SOARING*.

 **Mental Exercise**

What Do You Want to Accomplish in Life?
What's Your Dream?

Take some time, right now, to think about your answer and then write those ideas down. This exercise, like all the others in this book, is intended to help you accomplish your goals and dreams. Sometimes it can be challenging to answer such questions, but amazing things can happen when brain, pen, and paper work together! Just ask yourself, "What do I really, really, really want?"

Congratulations! Pat yourself on the back! By listing and committing to the ideas you put on paper, you have taken *the* key step in uncovering the power that can bring them to fruition. If you nonchalantly dismiss this exercise, strap that helmet back on and get back in the ball game. To succeed in life, you must first know what you want out of it! When you write a goal down, you're four times more likely to achieve it.

Look again at your answers. When you push yourself, you can accomplish them...and much more! Why? Countless studies have shown that we utilize only ten percent, or less, of our brains!

Considering man's great accomplishments, imagine what could be done if we would use even a small portion of the other 90 percent of our true potential! Even if we used only one percent more of our brain's capacity, that would still be a ten percent increase. That would be enough to put us way beyond what we ever thought possible! The truth is, our mental potential is literally unimaginable and way under used.

Mental Exercise

What Would You Do if You Had the Time and Money to Do Anything You Wanted to Do?

You may have asked yourself a similar question when you were a child. But have you asked it recently? If you're like most people, probably not. Maybe you weren't willing to invest the time. You may think there are more immediate and pressing things to think about. But take a moment, right now, to *seriously* consider this question, and write down the answer. What would you do if you could do anything? Absolutely *anything?* For example, you might say, "I would travel with my family and see the world." Or, "I would take my son or daughter to school every day." Perhaps you would say, "I would golf, sail, or play tennis a lot."

As a child, your entire life was in front of you. You probably had no major responsibilities, and believed you could be anything you wanted to be when you grew up. You may have wanted to be a doctor, an engineer, a fireman, a nurse, a pilot, a sea captain, or any number of things. You were a "child of unlimited potential."

Now, however, it's likely your view of the possibilities for your life has changed. You probably picked a direction for yourself and started down your chosen path. Inevitably, your focus became narrowed as you developed the specialized skills you needed for the occupation you chose. You may have become set in your ways, and perhaps you've stopped asking yourself questions like, "What do I *really* want to do with my life?" Now, your questions are more likely along the lines of, "What do I *have* to do today?"

Dreaming is usually easy when you're a child—your life, in most cases, is relatively simple and uncomplicated. Most of the routine details of everyday living are handled for you, giving you much more free time to play, pretend, explore, and dream. But now you're a busy "big" person with all sorts of challenges and responsibilities. Playtime has been reduced to a minimum. The pressures of living have replaced the pleasure of pretending. You're a grownup now, and not much seems to be the fun it was before.

But does it really have to be that way?

Child's Play

Let's go ahead and take some time to let go of the "restraints" of adulthood and play a "child's" game. Let's take a moment to pretend. It may be one of the most significant things you do in your adult life, as you begin to *SOAR* in the direction of your dreams. Here we go...

Seemingly, by accident, you've rediscovered the brass key for that dusty old treasure chest in your attic. You locked it up years ago and, over time, you'd forgotten all about it. The sparks igniting your memory tell you that this is no ordinary key—it's the key that will unlock your imagination and your dreams. It's the key to your personal "Hope Chest"! With exciting memories from the past racing through your mind, you bound up the stairs. You start remembering all the great stuff you used to store in that chest as a child.

Excited, you quickly unlock the chest and fling it wide open. You discover, to your amazement, all that remains is a dusty document lying beside a tarnished lamp—the prover-bial lamp with the genie inside.

Your recollection of what had been in the chest is gone. You dust off the document and read that the genie within the lamp is prepared to grant you your greatest wish. By freeing the genie, your deepest desires and dreams will be fulfilled. The document goes on to explain that, to release the genie, you must polish the lamp to its orignial luster.

Judging by the looks of the lamp, you realize it will take a great effort to wipe away the years of tarnish that have held the genie hostage. But once it's done, your life will be changed forever. Anything you wish for will be yours for the asking.

If asked, most of us wouldn't admit to closing the door on this kind of opportunity. But many do! *Somewhere, deep in-side each of us, a genie, known as our Potential, lies in wait.* Unfortunately, most of us are too preoccupied with surviving day by day to invest the time and effort required to release our genie to the world. As a result, most of us never realize even a fraction of our true potential.

Why is it that most people choose to keep this unlimited potential bottled up inside themselves? Are you one of those people? If so, what do you need to do to set it free and allow yourself the chance to create the life you desire and deserve?

The answer to this great "mystery" is surprisingly simple. And you already hold the key! The key is commitment—sustained commitment. The choices you make every day, and the time you take acting on them, reveal what you're committed to.

Mental Exercise
What Are You Committed to?

The choices you make determine the quality of your life. You choose what you do for a living, where you live, who your friends are, and how you spend your leisure time. Every day you decide when to wake up, what to eat, what to wear, and when to go to sleep. Every day you choose what your attitude is going to be. You choose what you're going to say and to whom you'll say it. You choose how you respond to events in your life. You choose what you believe in and what you value.

So many choices! What it comes down to is this:

You choose how you are going to live every day, which collectively makes up the weeks, months, and years of your life. Life is a kaleidoscope of never-ending choices. All of these choices, mixed together, are the ingredients of your meal ticket. Whether you serve yourself crash diet portions or a gourmet meal depends entirely on you.

The bottom line is, *you* choose your own level of success in life. Yes, *you!*

So then, what's your choice? Go ahead and write it down. Are you going to live the life you want or be swayed by the events of everyday living? Only you can decide. Remember, choice, not chance, determines your destiny.

The Smart Money Says...

There is no genetic master plan that predisposes some people to succeed and some to fail. The direction your life takes and how high you go is up to you.

Chapter 2

GO FOR IT!
WHAT'S HOLDING YOU BACK?

"Dare! And dare again! And go on daring."
George Danton

Do You Realize What You Have Your Hands On?
Why do so many dreamers, despite having good ideas or a great opportunity in their hands, sit idly by and go nowhere? Why don't they take off and start flying away to their dream? After all, even though they may not realize it, they're the pilot of their lives. They have the wings of success in their grasp. All they need to do is take off and fly.

I don't know anyone who doesn't someday want to land in Successville and take up residence. Yet, I know many people who have folded up their wings and decided to remain on the ground. There are a couple of reasons for this:

➤ They have allowed their *comfort zone* to entrap them.
➤ They haven't taken *responsibility* for their own lives.

There's Danger in the Comfort (Familiar) Zone
Someone once said, *"A ship in a harbor is safe. But that is not what ships were built for..."* For years, people have been using the term comfort zone. Yet, actually, your so-called comfort zone is often not comfortable at all—it's just familiar! For example, you may be working at a job that, day in and day out, is fairly predictable. You may like what you do but not like your boss, some of your co-workers, your work space, or your pay. If that's the case, *you're not really comfortable—are you?* Your situation is simply familiar.

Your natural tendency is to center your life inside your familiar zone, doing what you're accustomed to doing. In it, you keep familiar things—items, ideas, and behaviors that address your primary needs and help you feel safe, secure, and loved, even if you aren't. Your familiar zone is comprised of things you can exert at least a measure of influence over, usually with predictable results—your job, your family and friends, and your activities.

Familiar zones may seem warm and fuzzy, like an old Teddy bear. However, they're also dangerous if you allow them to be an excuse to prevent you from moving on to a happy, fulfilled, prosperous life. Extend yourself and take the chances necessary for you to activate your potential and succeed in a big way.

Let go of whatever non-productive thinking, behavior (habits), and other things that might be holding you back. It requires courage to cut the tether and venture out toward your dream, and that's what you need to do to create the life you want. The "FUD" (Fear, Uncertainty, and Doubt) factor comes into play any time you make a decision to take off from the ground—the familiar zone to which you've grown accustomed.

Remember how you felt when, as a child, you left your friends behind and moved to a new neighborhood, attended a new school, or did something else that took you away? The temporary feelings of disorientation and uncertainty, which come from facing the unknown, are temporary. Yet many people strive to avoid them for the rest of their lives.

Unfortunately, the cost of staying safe often results in the loss of success. As Dale Carnegie once said, *"All life is a chance, so take it! The person who goes furthest is the one who is willing to do and dare."*

Feel the Fear and Take Off Anyway!

As the philosopher Goethe once said, *"What you can do, or dream you can do, begin it; boldness has genius, power, and magic in it."* By answering the following questions, you'll learn a lot about yourself and how you tend to react to the idea of taking a risk.

📑 Mental Exercise

Take Some Time to Think About Your Answer
and Observe Your Feelings.

➤ How do you feel when you consider the changes that will result in your life when you make your dreams come to life and become your new reality?

➤ How do you feel when you consider the prospect of changing jobs?

➤ What are your feelings about going for it—doing whatever it takes to make it happen?

Are You Afraid?

Are you afraid to let go of your present situation and move on from what you already have, even though you may currently be heading in a direction that offers little promise? Does the idea of changing and going in a different direction scare you to death?

Are your dreams big enough to drive you to overcome your fear, to _SOAR_ and achieve the life you've always wanted for yourself and your family?

You may be relieved to know there are no right or wrong answers to these questions. Your answers just reflect where you are right now in your thinking. As you continue to grow, your inner changes will become evident in your outer world. This is where following a personal development program of books, tapes, and seminars comes in. We all need to change our inner world to live our dreams.

Do You Feel Hesitant?

Do you understand the value of building your career or business so you can create a brighter future? Or, are you placing just as much value on your current source of income—which you may consider a sure thing—just because it enables you to pay the mortgage and car payments?

Are You Excited?

Do you feel fired up—passionate and invigorated by the possibilities that taking a new direction in your life could bring? Do you welcome the changes and challenges ahead?

Most people admit to falling into one of the first two categories. Fear, the most debilitating of all our emotions, serves as "magnetic north" in guiding the course most people take through life. If this is true for you, the great news is you can break through the fear and turn your dreams into reality.

Staying Stuck Is Limiting

Are you staying stuck at a job you don't like because you're afraid of not being able to pay the bills? Do you avoid introducing yourself to people you'd like to meet because you're afraid of rejection? Most people let their fear keep them grounded, preventing them from looking out over the horizon and seeing the possibilities for their lives. How about you?

Your familiar zone tends to narrow your perspective. For example, some people spend more time worrying about how they're going to pay off their credit cards rather than how they could double their income! Most people resort to the Rip Van Winkle approach when confronted with turning-point decisions: "Let me sleep on it, and in 20 years I'll wake up and do it!" This is one time where it pays to be a member of the "out" crowd.

So, to broaden your perspective, you need to venture out of your familiar zone, which often means associating with more positive thinking people—others who are moving on too.

> ### In Life, There's No Such Thing as "Instant Replay"

Dr. Anthony Compolo conducted a study in which 50 people over the age of 95 were asked: *"If you could live your life over again, what would you do differently?"*

The top three answers were:
> I'd reflect more.
> I'd risk more.
> I'd do more things that would live on after I am gone.

We can all learn from the wisdom of the ages—*and the aged.* I've spoken with a number of retired people who have devoted their entire careers to "Old Faithful, Inc." Their lives are filled with unfulfillment and regret, and they often reflect on the things they've always dreamed of doing in their lives. Like everyone else caught up in "The Rat Race," they did only what they needed to do to get around the next corner.

Meanwhile, time marched forward and their dreams evaporated. *Most people tend to put off living. They dream of winning the lottery instead of doing whatever it takes to live their dream.* Treasure being alive now. Diligently build your dream and work toward it.

It's sad most people don't think more of themselves and their ability to make great things happen in their lives. Often they immerse themselves in the negative news on TV and in the newspaper. They *passively* allow the "disaster du jour" (disaster of the day) to be their focus instead of their dreams! They allow such negativity to weigh them down. Often they end up in a downward spiral of negativity. They lose faith in the world, in themselves, and in their ability to make their dreams come true.

If you relate to any or all of this, it's time to take charge and revive your dreams and ambitions! Fortunately, more and more people are waking up to the emptiness of their lives and taking action. For example, the network marketing industry has been a strong influence in this area—giving people hope and a vehicle with which to achieve their dreams.

The only real doom and gloom I see is the fact that many people are swallowing these spoonsful of negativity and have stopped doing whatever it takes to achieve their dreams! That, to me, is the greatest tragedy of all! Many people's perspectives are being blind-sided by the negativity prevalent in today's society. They see themselves as mere pebbles on the massive beachfront of humanity. They see themselves incapable of mustering a ripple, let alone a wave, in the tumultuous sea of complex, fast-paced, and ever changing times. The fact is, they need to get beyond this minimizing thinking and learn to *SOAR.*

When you're taking off for your dream, it's best to press play and turn on a positive tape, read a positive book, or go to an invigorating seminar. Don't spend your precious time watching or reading the negative news or seeing TV shows that don't support you and your dream. Truly successful people know they need to *invest* their time in developing themselves. (Notice I said *invest* time—not spend time. Your greatest investment is in yourself.) They know that to get to the next level of their career or business, they need to grow and become the best they can be.

To change your life, you may need to change some habits! To maximize your personal growth, as you build your career or business, feed yourself with positive information instead of negative information. It's one of the keys of success. Duplicate what leaders do, rather than later wishing you could have an instant replay of these valuable years of your life. Get and stay excited! Enthusiasm makes a difference. Stay fired up about your dream and help others get fired up about theirs!

Rationalizing (Telling Yourself *Rational-Sounding Lies*) Doesn't Pay

I often hear people rationalizing their lack of drive and commitment to succeed. They have excuses like, "I know I could make it happen if I just had more money to work with...or knew the right people...or had more time...or...or..." What a shame!

Who knows what great accomplishments lie buried beneath the ironclad will of life's procrastinators? Imagine how different our lives would be if people like Thomas Edison, Abraham Lincoln, Rosa Parks, the Wright Brothers, and Christopher Columbus had taken the wisdom of their day to heart?

You need to fight the gravitational pull of fear as you venture outside your comfort zone; after all, being creatures of habit and comfort, this goes against our nature! Your failure to fight fear can result in lifestyle paralysis and can lead to dependencies that restrict your options.

🐱 Mental Exercise

Achiever Profile: *So, You Think You're Busy? Then Think About This.*

Once a daughter of a former President of the United States spent three years writing a book. During this time, she managed to graduate from law school, pass the bar exam, and give birth to two children. Asked how she was able to write a book and juggle all of these things, she shrugged, "Just work at it, a little bit every day." Sure she was busy "taking care of business." But not so busy that she lost sight of her dreams. The price of dreams isn't cheap—that's what makes them so precious!

Contrary to most people's beliefs, fulfilling your responsibilities and achieving your dreams aren't mutually exclusive unless you say so! Everyone chooses their own lot in life. No matter what they're involved in, have you noticed that *people always seem to find time for the things that truly matter to them?*

To discover your true potential, you need to develop a test-pilot mentality and push yourself "outside of the envelope." You need to go beyond the artificial boundaries of apprehension and obligation that prevent most people from living their dream. You need to be hungry enough for your dream before you can be more and do more. It takes working diligently and smartly, focusing on your dreams and goals. It also requires having a driving passion for wanting the best—without compromise—for yourself and those you care about. Only then will you ever seriously attempt to break out of your familiar zone and stretch your horizons. As Robert Louis Stevenson once said, *"Wherever we are, it is but a stage on the way to somewhere else, and whatever we do, however well we do it, it is only a preparation to do something else that shall be different."*

Okay, now ask yourself one more question:

Mental Exercise

What's the Worst Thing that Could Possibly Happen if You Left Your Comfort (Familiar) Zone and Decided to Pursue Your Ultimate Dream Right Now?

Let's say the worst actually happened. Would you settle for it and quit chasing your dreams, content in knowing you had tried, or would you turn up the flame a bit and press on?

If the worst did happen, would you— *turn the flame off and say goodbye to your dreams or turn up the flame and make them come true?*

DARE GREATLY...

"It is not the critic
who counts; nor the man
who points out how the strong
man stumbled, or where the doer
of deeds could have done better. The
credit belongs to the man who is actually in the arena; whose face is marred by
dust and sweat and blood; who strives val-
iantly; who errs and comes short again and
again; who knows the great enthusiasms,
great devotions, and spends himself in a
worthy cause; who at the best knows in
the end the triumph of high achievement; and who at the worst, if he
fails, at least fails while daring
greatly; so that his place shall
never be with those cold and
timid souls who know
neither victory
nor defeat."

Theodore Roosevelt

Chapter 3

SELF-RESPONSIBILITY
STAY ON COURSE—
NO MATTER WHAT

"It's up to you to make your dream come true!"
Robert H. Schuller

Is Your Ladder of Success Leaning Against the Wrong Wall?

It's sad to say, but surveys show that around seventy percent of the working population hates going to work. Are you one of them? These people are climbing the ladder of success, and finding that it's leaning against the wrong wall.

For example, let's take someone working at a fast food restaurant who wants to be wealthy and have more options in their life. If they keep serving burgers and fries but don't further their education, training, and experience, they'll never get what they want. They need to start doing whatever it takes to become a manager and then an owner, to make their dreams come true.

The problem is most people lack a simple method for directing their energies and monitoring their progress in pursuit of their dream. Next to being in the wrong vehicle to start with, this is the single biggest reason people lose their way en-route to making their dreams come true.

Expanding your horizons and soaring to success doesn't happen overnight, though—it's an ongoing process. Your dreams and goals are achieved through personal growth, regular intervals of evaluation and, when necessary, course corrections. Self-responsibility is accountability. It's absolutely essential so you can keep heading in the direction you've chosen, and not allow yourself to get blown off course.

Jay Rifenbary, in his best-selling book titled *No Excuse!*, said the following about self-responsibility: "As you accept responsibility for your actions, you will likely live life with a lighter heart." Knowing you have deliberately decided not to blame others for your actions, you will feel stronger, less alone, and less frightened of the consequences. The fear of rejection and failure that once crippled or handicapped your efforts will diminish. You are taking charge.

The likelihood that you'll let fear control or paralyze your actions will be reduced. Your self-responsibility can develop as you grow personally and begin to live more of your dream.

In my talks and group discussions, I illustrate the importance of a self-responsibility system by comparing it to a journey along a stretch of a major highway.

Picture yourself excited about where you're going while driving down an unfamiliar highway with no road signs. You've been traveling several hours and have driven past a series of interchanges and exits, all without identifying signs. How would you know if you're still going in the right direction toward your destination?

Over time, you lose your sense of perspective. You ask yourself, "Am I anywhere close to my destination? Have I taken a wrong turn along the way, gone past my exit, or not gone far enough?" Reaching your destination, in this instance, would depend more on luck—mere happenstance—than skill!

The same holds true as you travel down the road toward your dreams and aspirations. You need a way, a self-responsibility system, to help you monitor your progress. You need to be alerted where to make a turn or change lanes and where to exit to land you in Successville.

It also serves another important role—it shines a guiding light on the path you need to take and helps you focus on the goals you've set. Keep your goals and dreams in front of you, and the big picture in sight, as you overcome the challenges of everyday life.

The MDT Self-Responsibility System

Earlier in life, most of us were influenced by the most exhausting and exacting system ever developed—the MDT Self-Responsibility System! Most of us made it through our early years in school primarily due to the preachings and teachings of—you probably guessed it—Mom, Dad, and Teacher (MDT).

Mom and Dad, or other people who took the role of your parents, were probably always there to wake you up in the morning and shuttle you off to school. Your teachers constantly did their best to "make your day" by giving you homework deadlines. Together, the parent/teacher teams exerted their influence to get you to achieve a set of goals collectively known as learning.

And learn you did, often whether you wanted to or not! With the MDT self-responsibility factors working in almost an autopilot mode, there was little opportunity for you to drift far off course during your first few years of education.

But as you grew older and may have been somewhat rebellious as a teenager, it's likely these self-responsibility factors became less significant in your life. Motivation became more of an "inside job," and you relied increasingly upon yourself. And, if you're like most people, you began accomplishing less and less.

George Will, the witty political commentator turned baseball writer, says that in baseball—*"Success goes to those who are paying attention, day by day, from April to October"*—the American baseball season.

The same holds true for you and me, except that our success season is January 1st to December 31st! Success is a continuing process that requires consistent effort.

The Smart Money Says...

 *When we become self-responsible, we move ourselves into a group of more highly developed individuals. They know they have only one shot at experiencing life, they understand it's a do-it-yourself opportunity, and they're determined to make the most of it.*

Are You Ready?

The purpose of *SOAR* is to get you into the habit of thinking success on a daily basis. *SOAR* is about developing a personal responsibility plan; it is about becoming serious, once and for all, about succeeding. *SOAR* is a self-responsibility system you can plug yourself into at any time. So, now is the time to be serious about achieving your dreams and goals! Choose a direction, an aim, a mission, a cause...and go for it! You'll be amazed at how much fun it can be, and you'll quickly get to know that bottled-up genie I've referred to as your potential.

Though this program is rather easy to understand and follow, success is a cumulative process—not an overnight ticket to the stars. There's no such thing as an overnight success—it takes time. Also, truly successful people often appear as ducks. They seem to be gliding effortlessly across the water, while they're vigorously paddling their webbed feet below the surface! As famous football coach Vince Lombardi once said, *"Inches make a champion."* Remember that no matter how long your journey is, it begins with a single step.

As you begin to *SOAR*, you'll start looking at the person in the mirror a bit differently. Instead of just seeing someone brushing his or her teeth, you will see the reflection of a person who desires more than routine everyday survival! You'll see a person with a zest for life—a person who's fired up—who sees the great opportunity they have to live the life they want to live. You'll see a person who dares to dream big dreams...and makes them happen!

Consider even the greatest of personally developed people—those with a thorough list of goals and action plans who are passionate about making a difference in their lives and the lives of others. Even they need directions to stay on the path of champions. It's not only those of you who are just getting started building your career or business.

Regardless of where you are in your personal growth, your life is in your own hands, and what you choose to make of it is entirely up to you. If you're serious about succeeding, *SOAR*'s simple approach can help you make some dramatic things happen for yourself. But, again, it's all up to you!

H.G. Wells once noted, *"The best measure of success in life is the ratio of our accomplishments to our capabilities."* How about you? Are you maximizing your capabilities? Are you stretching yourself? Do you want more than you are getting out of life?

Decide now to make things happen. Decide now that, even if you don't know how to do something, you'll begin anyway and learn as you go. Decide now to live up to your potential. Decide now to live life like it was meant to be lived.

Successful living—getting what you want out of life—is first a matter of choice, then doing everything you can to make it a reality. What's *your* choice? What are you going to do?

Dare to SOAR! Let's move on to the chapters covering *SEEING, ORGANIZING, ACTING,* and *REJECTING*—which show you how to do it!

Chapter 4

SEEING IS BELIEVING!
START BY SEEING YOUR
GOALS AND DREAMS

*"Before you begin a thing, remind yourself
that difficulties and delays quite impossible to foresee
lie ahead—you can only see one thing clearly and that is
your goal. Form a mental vision of that and
cling to it through thick and thin."*
Kathleen Norris

Can You *SEE* Your Success?

Your journey of success begins simply enough—with goals and dreams. To varying degrees, we all have goals. Some people, however, are much more successful than others in achieving them. Why? Because goal achievers have developed tremendous ability to *SEE* their success—the *S* in *SOAR*. And you can do it too.

When you take a goal and run it through this crucial first step of *SOAR*—*SEEing*—sparks start flying and things begin to happen. When you start to fill in the lines and begin adding the colors of the exciting images that represent your goals and dreams, the magic power of your passion takes over! This is *SEEING*.

SEEING is using your mind, or your mind's eye as some people call it, to visualize the successful completion of your goals. *SEEING* is first watching yourself succeed mentally—before you actually do it in reality.

SEEING success in your mind is a very important—and very powerful—first step toward achieving your goals. To succeed, you first need to *believe* you can. *SEEING* helps you condition your mind into a framework of positive thinking and helps you focus on doing the things that will make you a winner. Invest time in *SEE-ING* on a regular basis, playing your future success scenes over and over in your mind. Soon they'll become so real to you that you'll believe your success is inevitable. And for people who make a habit of dreaming and acting on those dreams—doing whatever it takes to make them come true—it is!

You may be familiar with Dr. Stephen R. Covey's best-selling book, *The 7 Habits of Highly Effective People.* Covey's second habit is—Begin with the End in Mind. He explains that *"All things are created twice. There's a mental or first creation, and a physical or second creation...."* Here we're talking about the mental creation.

Successful people use *SEEING*—Covey's first creation. It shapes their thinking and subsequently their lives. One of the most dramatic examples of turning *SEEING* into success occurred at the 1991 World Track and Field Championships in Tokyo.

A True Leap of Faith

Mike Powell was only four years old when Bob Beamon recorded a world-record long jump of 29 feet, 2.5 inches at the 1968 Olympics in Mexico City. Along the line, Powell got the dream to beat Beamon's record jump. Thirteen years later, on his second to last jump of the day, Powell raised the world record mark to 29 feet, 4.5 inches! In an instant, he had turned what some would consider his unrealistic dream into reality. In the process, he accomplished three significant things:

1. He broke the longest-standing individual record in track and field—one that many experts believed might *never* be broken!
2. He broke the 65-meet winning streak of Carl Lewis who, despite having achieved the four longest jumps of his life at the same meet in Tokyo, lost for the *first* time in over a decade!
3. He broke his own personal record by nearly a foot!

But for Mike Powell, becoming a sudden hero, an overnight success, as some would say, required *years* of perseverance. "All my life," Powell said, "I've had people tell me I couldn't do certain things." But you might ask, "So how did he *SOAR* above the nay-sayers?" Are you ready for his secret?

He did it by *SEEING* himself making that record-shattering jump! He pictured it in his mind *over* and *over* again. In his *Sports Illustrated* magazine feature article, Bruce Newman eloquently described Powell's mental practice:

> He would sit all alone in his living room, often for hours at a time, waiting until the daylight had drained out of the walls, and the room was cool and dark. That way he could see the dream better, as if it were a movie whose image fades in the light. When the hairs finally began to stand up on the back of his neck, Mike Powell would walk slowly to the back of the house, turn, then wait until he could see it squarely in front of him again.
>
> He would come bounding out of the TV room, turn left after he passed through the foyer, then make another sharp left as he entered the living room. "By the time I got to the dining room I would jump, and I would visualize myself breaking the world record," Powell says.
>
> "Sometimes I would just be sitting there on his couch, and all of a sudden here came Mike," says Karen Koellner, Powell's girlfriend of three years. "He would come running through his living room, take off, then the minute he landed he'd throw his hands in the air and start jumping up and down. He always mentally broke the record. Every single time."
>
> Powell never deprived himself of the elation the moment would bring. "I could actually feel it, feel the rush in my head," he says. "I've imagined that moment in my living room a hundred times...."

Now *that's* dreaming—that's what I mean by *SEEING*. That's the kind of dreaming most of us did as children. It's the kind of *SEEING* most of us need to do a lot more of as adults. *SOARING* to success begins with the dream. Add hearing and feeling your dream to *SEEING* it, and you'll have a powerful combination that'll help you take action to make it a reality.

SEEING Is Believing—*in Yourself!*

Great achievements begin with the ability to *SEE* the possibilities you want to create in your life. *SEEING* is mental dreaming—dream building in your mind—if you will. It's about stretching your imagination and visualizing yourself arriving in Successville (whatever and wherever that is for you) is taking your coat off and staying for awhile. It all boils down to believing in yourself as you achieve your goals! This keeps you motivated and producing.

People become great, not because of superior genes or astronomical intellects, but, first of all, because of their ability to *SEE* that life has a limitless number of possibilities. They choose a goal, believe in it, and commit themselves to it. Sure, they may be afraid, but they do it *anyway.* And once they get started their fear diminishes. They *totally* commit themselves to it.

Successful people *SEE* through the clouds of doubt and uncertainty that most people view as obscuring the top. Instead, their perspective is one of *rainbows.* They shift from Murphy's Law which says, "If anything can go wrong, it will," to The Success Law that says, "*If anything can go right, it will!*" They see the glass as not only being half-full, but ready to be filled to the very top.

Neil Armstrong, the first man to walk on the moon, dreamed, as a little boy, of someday doing something important in aviation. But do you think, as a little boy, he ever imagined himself walking on the moon? Some people would say, "that's ridiculous"—a word the "experts" are particularly fond of using—right? "A man walking on the moon? Children say the silliest things sometimes. That's crazy."

Regardless of what people thought, Neil Armstrong changed history forever when he took that *"One small step for man, one giant leap for mankind."* He didn't let the negative-thinking people get him down.

Do You Dream Big Enough in Your Life?

Most people don't; they're just getting by day-to-day. Unfortunately, they limit their dreams to what they think is realistic. They look at their history, at their own lack of success in the past, and base their expectations on that. They believe what the so-called experts think is probable. What's *realistic* for you is simply whatever you *believe*—simply whatever you SEE for yourself!

Neil Armstrong, and people like him, dream, not only of the possible but also the impossible! Remember, so-called experts are only one level above a critic on the "food chain." "Friends," who are supposedly concerned about you and only looking out for your best interests, fall somewhere in between. The questions you need to ask yourself are, "Who's responsible for my life?" and "Who pays my bills?" The answer, of course, is *you—not* your friends, relatives, or acquaintances.

Hubert Humphrey is regarded by many as one of the greatest U.S. Vice Presidents in history. Early on, Humphrey wrote a letter to his wife after visiting Washington, D.C. for the first time: *"I can see how, if you and I just apply ourselves and make up our minds for bigger things, we can...live here in Washington and probably be in government, politics, or public service. Oh gosh, I hope my dreams come true. I'm going to do my best anyhow."*

Wishful thinking on Hubert's part? *After all*, he wasn't even in the political arena yet. Most people probably would've said his ideas were pretty far-fetched at the time he wrote the letter. But Humphrey and history proved otherwise.

Great achievements begin with great dreams. T.E. Lawrence (of Arabia) said there are two types of dreamers in this world:

*"Those who dream in the quiet hours of their sleep and those
who dream in the waking hours of their day. Night dreamers
discard their dreams as mere fantasy when they awaken.
Whereas, those who dream in the day are ready to breathe action into their dreams and turn them into reality."*

Daytime dreamers *SEE* the true potential of their dreams:
They *SEE* themselves succeeding at events that lay years in the
future. They *SEE* the truth in advance!

Successful daytime dreamers are goal dreamers. They know it
is only people with the vision to *SEE* their goals and dreams who
make great contributions to mankind.

Ask yourself, "What kind of a dreamer am I?" What kind of
dreamer do you *want* to be? Walt Disney once said, *"If you can
dream it, you can do it!"* And you can! Take time right now to
play the role of a great achiever—the role of a winner, who
makes their dreams come alive by *SEEING* them first!

🔲 Mental Exercise

***Picture Yourself Accomplishing Something
You Really, Really Want to Do***

Is it building a business that spans the globe so you can enjoy
financial freedom? Is it rising to the top in your career? How
about having the time and money to travel with your family
anywhere in the world and to be able to stay as long as you
want? Do you want to build a dream home? What would it look
like? Would you simply like to enjoy more time with your family at home? Do you want to go fishing more, buy a boat, have a
vacation home, or what? Write down your answers.

Now develop this picture in your mind, go a step farther,
making it come alive as much as possible. What are you hearing? What do you see, feel, and smell around you? The more
real you make it in your mind, the greater your chances are of

turning it into reality! Write down what you're *SEEING* (feeling, hearing, and smelling). How does it feel to be succeeding and on top of the world? Are you excited? The more fired up you are about your dream, the more likely you are to live it!

Practice, Practice, Practice!

Dream building can be fun, but it's important to take it seriously. It's an essential part of your success. You need to commit yourself regularly to put time into your schedule to dream. The deeper your commitment to do this, the deeper your passion for your dream will become. You need to make it a habit of *SEEING* your success daily.

Sure you're a busy person—most everyone is. Sure you've got a lot to do! You may feel you'd like to have more hours in the day. I often feel the same way. But if you *really* want to succeed, take a step back and *invest* some time in *SEEING*. It's the first step to *SOARING*, and it's a big one—it lays the foundation upon which you build the rest of your life! All you really need is a little time every day to unwind and let your mind and body relax. Give yourself time to *SEE*.

Is succeeding a priority for you? If so, make it your goal to *SEE* success 35 minutes a week—*just five minutes a day*. If you want to change your life, you need to change your thoughts first! The truth is 35 minutes of a 168-hour week is really not that much. We all have time for that! In fact, it's amazing how, when we invest that 35 minutes in dreaming and goal setting, the other 167 hours and 25 minutes of the week are significantly enhanced! That's a big payoff for such a small effort!

How committed are you to doing what you may have secretly wanted to do for years? Are you really going to make it happen? You can you know, you really can.

Block out the pressures that are part of everyday living and *SEE* yourself win! Create a story line of the life you want to live and watch it happen for you! Your creative juices will really start pumping as you visualize yourself doing the exciting things you've always dreamed of.

SEEING yourself succeeding has a rippling effect that spills over into a positive mental attitude. First, your mind's eye *SEES* success. And, after a while, it believes it. Reality may not be far behind, as long as you consistently work toward it.

Incorporate the following six tips into your dreaming exercises, and your goals will develop a power of their own. Let them be your "*SEEING* I" Guide.

Tip #1: Relax Your Mind!

To begin with, you need to be relaxed to *SEE* clearly. Put the mental clutter of daily pressures and to-do lists on a shelf—somewhere out of your mind's reach. In order to *wonder,* your mind first needs time to *wander.*

Relaxation takes many different forms. Some people dream best in the evening, reclined in a quiet room, away from children and ringing phones. Then there are those who *SEE* most clearly in the morning, under a hot shower.

I unwind by exercising. Granted, exercise isn't the first thing that comes to mind when most people think about relaxing. But we're talking about relaxing the mind, and a good physical workout really works! A good workout can be as simple as a brisk 30-minute walk. Or you may prefer to ride a stationary bike, jog, or run.

After my heart rate is up and my muscles are warm and functioning smoothly, my mind begins to wonder. I find myself reaching levels of creativity my conscious mind would never otherwise get to.

Many people who jog regularly report that some of their best and brightest ideas came to them in the middle of a run, seemingly out of the blue. In fact, the acronym *SOAR* came to me one day halfway through a 30-minute jog. Stimulation of the heart and muscles can set your mental sparks flying and generate a surplus of fresh ideas.

Is there something you've always wanted to do, but never took action on? What would you need to do in order to go for it? Do you really want to build your career or business and make it happen? Or do you just want to make enough additional money to take a nice vacation every year? How? Start with open-ended thoughts or questions, and whittle away at them as you play them over in your mind. After awhile, you'll have sculpted a mental picture masterpiece, and the miles on the jogging or walking path will *SOAR* by!

Tip #2: Establish a Routine

Keep your dreams in plain sight of your mind's eye by making your dream time a regular part of your routine. At first, it requires constant effort to create this or any habit. Once you create it though, you can keep each dream alive, until you achieve it, for the rest of your life. Habits die hard, and when you make dreaming a

habit, your dreams will never die!

Each Sunday evening around 9 p.m., I set some time aside for *SEEING*—both future goals and successes to be found in the coming week. I disappear into my home office and quietly let my mind race through the maze that holds the answers for reaching my goals. Through regular *SEEING* sessions, smaller achievements become ordinary, and large achievements get closer and closer.

The key is to *make SEEING a part of your regular schedule.* You can't realistically expect to improve your physical appearance and wellbeing through sporadic exercise. The same holds true when you're exercising your mind! Pick a time each day or each week that works best for you and stick to it! It's best to choose a time when distractions are at a minimum, your schedule is clear, and you don't have an appointment you need to rush off to.

Tip #3: The Fun Factor—*What Fires Your Enthusiasm?*
If you find yourself having difficulties focusing on your *SEEING*, start with those things which most interest you. It can be your family, a hobby you enjoy, traveling, a sport you'd like to engage in, going to a certain level in your career or business—whatever fires you up the most!

I might dream of walking up to the 72nd hole of the U.S. Open Golf Championship with a two-shot lead over the immortal "Golden Bear" himself, Jack Nicklaus. In my mind, I see myself...strolling up the fairway of the last hole with the gallery—ten people deep—lining each side.

I feel the tension grip my limbs as I take my final back swing of the day...knocking my ball safely onto the green 20 feet from the hole. Sheer exhilaration surges through my body! Two putts later, my ball resting peacefully in the cup, I raise my putter into the air as the gallery roars its approval. It's over! The amateur has come from out of nowhere to shock the golfing world and one of its legends!

Every time I think of my dream game with Jack, I catch myself smiling. For me, this would be funny! Fantasy? Most certainly. One thing's for sure—I always feel good about myself after *SEEING* events like this one. That in itself is a big plus! You can *SEE* something you're passionate about *and* committed to following through with, to create that reality in your life. That way you have a feel good, and a great dream to *SOAR* after. That would be a powerful combination, wouldn't it?

What does it for you? What do you *really, really, really* want? What would you love to do if you knew you had only a short time to live? Is it going to a certain level in your career or business?

For instance, can you see yourself and your spouse all dressed up, going across the stage to accept an award, along with some flowers, at a business function? Can you hear your favorite music playing? Can you hear the cheers of the people in the audience and their loud applause that keeps on going for several minutes? Can you see yourself at the podium, telling *your* story, inspiring others that you did it and they can too?

I'm here to tell you right now that you *can* make it happen—whatever "it" is for you. You need to *SEE* it first though, as specifically as possible. This'll help you believe that it *can* happen for you. You *can SOAR*, no matter how many times you've failed to do so in the past. Lots of people have done it and you can too!

Expand your dreams to include financial wealth, being at your goal weight and radiantly healthy, purchasing a summer home in the mountains—whatever it is that you like. *SEEING* is fun—and you're the boss! By starting with fun things that spark your greatest enthusiasm, your dreaming will begin to build your sense of self-worth. It will extend into the rest of your thinking—*and will be reflected in your life!*

Tip #4: Dump the Doubt and *Power Dream*

Henry Ford, whose profound visions of transportation and manufacturing sparked explosive advances and turned societal norms on their ear, said something that has always stuck with me: *"Whether you think you can or you think you can't, you're right!"* Ford realized the only limits people of his age encounter are those they, perhaps without even realizing it, set for themselves. No matter how sophisticated and technologically adept we have become, some things about us will never change.

Nothing dilutes the potency of a powerful dream more than doubt. Doubt is the biggest dreamstealer of all. Shed the restraints of skepticism like, "I don't have the brains, money, or connections to make it to the top." Wipe your mental slate clean. From here on out, you're only looking forward! Like all of us, you've made some mistakes in the past. But now you are making a conscious choice to learn what you can from them and move on to the life you've always dreamed of living.

What do you really want to do with *your* life? What do you want to be when you "grow up"? Adults probably asked you that as a child, and you need to ask it of yourself. A wealthy land owner? A recreational pilot? The inventor of a new game? The owner of a successful business? A philanthropist? Forget what your current situation looks like—what do you *SEE* for yourself in *your future?*

Your dreams are yours for the taking. Claim them. Take charge! Nothing else can give you that great feeling of aliveness, the sparkle in your eyes, or the tremendous satisfaction and growth you'll experience as, one by one, you make your dreams come true.

Sure, maybe you inherited some money and could buy one of your dreams. That's all well and good. There's nothing wrong with that. But, don't let anyone kid you—it's *not* the same as "taking the bull by the horns." Turn the TV off, get up from your comfortable chair or couch, or from playing at your computer, and do what you need to do to build your career or business. No one else will do it for you.

Nothing compares with the happiness and fulfillment you'll feel when you take charge of your future. Little by little, each day you're moving closer and closer to your dream. Your life just lights up and your spirit *SOARS.* You'll know, deep in your heart, that, by golly, you *are* making it happen, *no matter what!*

There are so many people out there who need your example of being a Power Dreamer. How do you think your leaders and heroes got where they are? It didn't happen by accident, that's for sure. They, in all likelihood, are "Power Dreamers."

What if they *hadn't* taken charge and made it happen? Would they have significantly, and positively, affected so many people? Of course not! What if they had said that they'd really rather stretch out on the couch and watch TV, and see *other* people succeed and earn a lot of money, rather than turn their life around by the power of their dreams?

Great leaders are courageous and visionary. We have them, and other such master dreambuilders, to thank for daring to *SOAR*. They claimed their dreams and helped others realize their own potential through power dreaming and taking action. Every time such people achieve their dream, they power dream a *bigger* dream and keep on *SOARING!*

As a child visiting an amusement park, you probably headed for the most attractive horse on the merry-go-round. It's not surprising that, as an adult, your mind takes you back to the childlike state of wonder when you allow yourself to dream about what you truly want to be, do, and have. As you find yourself getting excited—as you open the door of your mind to consider your possibilities—*you're on the right track to ultimate success, whatever that means for you.*

In this great big world of ours, having a rich life experience, however *you* define that for yourself and your family, is realistic. And remember what's realistic for you is whatever you *believe*. Strengthen your belief. Make the powerful dream in your head move into your heart and into your life.

You're learning to go beyond your familiar zone and reach for the sky. Your dream is the wind beneath your wings that lifts you up and carries you from your present reality to the life you've been *SEEING*. Take off and *SOAR!*

Tip #5: Draw Vivid Mental Pictures

While dreaming of golf, I might visualize myself standing tall and taking a smooth swing that launches my ball 285 yards down the middle of the fairway. I watch its flight...nice high arch, straight, and long.

In other areas of my life, I'm also drawing vivid pictures in my mind—mental pictures in which I'm winning, accomplishing, laughing, and loving. I can't over-emphasize the importance of this!

Draw vivid pictures of your dreams in your mind and mentally act out scenarios in which you're creating big wins. This will inject you with increased self-confidence and resourcefulness. Bring the details into focus: Imagine the sights, smells, and sounds around you as you find your way to the top—to the pinnacle of your success, wherever that is for you. Remember, it's *your* life and *your* dream we're talking about here.

The more detailed and vivid these pictures are in your mind, the more realistic your chances of achieving your dreams are going to be. In a very real sense, you're programming your mind for success. Dream of success scenarios and focus on the smallest details that make the gap between your dream and your reality smaller and smaller—until it disappears altogether! Your mind becomes convinced what you really want can indeed happen for you. And anything you set your mind to, you can accomplish.

Mike Powell drew vivid mental pictures of his world-record-breaking long jump. He even went so far as to act the jump out in his dream by running through the house and leaping across the living room! Some people might find that kind of behavior peculiar. But they didn't break a 23-year-old world record either. Mike Powell did. He has already *SOARED* high and far, and it remains to be seen how much higher and farther the power of his dreams can take him.

Start mastering your ability to dream vividly by taking a few moments to do the exercises at the end of this chapter. Discovering your dreams and then picturing yourself as having already achieved them are two key steps toward actually making them a part of your life. *SEE* yourself as a winner—as a can-doer! Dreaming in this manner will give you the *lift* you need to *SOAR!* Others have done it and you can too.

Tip #6: Put Your Dreams on Paper
In 1953 a study was done at Yale Law School to determine the power that writing down goals had on eventual success. The

law students were asked questions about their goals. Although most of the class was able to verbally state their future expectations, it was discovered that only *three percent* had written their goals down on paper. Twenty years later, these students were tracked down, and a survey was done to determine the level of success they had attained. It was discovered that the *three* percent who had written their goals down achieved more financial and personal success than the remaining 97 percent of their class *put together*!

Writing your goals and dreams on paper, and frequently referring to them to keep you on track, is one of the things that separates the *dreamers* from the *doers*. As mentioned earlier, success is a cumulative process that happens one step at a time. And the first step involves developing a dream and writing it down!

Tip #7: Keep Your Dreams in Front of You

Keep your written dreams in a place where they'll serve as a constant reminder to you. This could be on the refrigerator or on a bulletin board in your office—anywhere you'll see them on a daily basis. *SEEING* your dreams in front of you on paper sparks your memory and serves as the proverbial carrot on a stick. It helps you stay accountable for the things necessary to accomplish your dreams.

You can stay excited about your dream more easily when you have pictures of it where you'll see it each day. For example, say you want to golf on the best courses around the world. Find a magazine that pictures them, cut out the pictures, and put them in places like your refrigerator, your bathroom mirror, at your desk, in your car, in your day planner or date book, and other places where you'll see them regularly.

What May Be Distracting You from Your Dream?

Are you so busy, just getting through the activities you believe you *have* to do, that you haven't been investing time on your dream? Are you rushing from home-to-work—squeezing in errands at lunch, then dashing from work-to-home—only to make or have a quick supper and scoot out the door again chauffeuring your children back and forth to their activities? Or, have you committed yourself to some volunteer activities in the evening or on weekends, like coaching soccer, heading a committee for the Parent Teacher Organization at school, or something else?

You may feel "roped in" to your current hectic schedule and believe you would be faced with some unhappy children, parents, or teachers if you stop doing what they expect you to do. Besides, isn't it just easier to not upset the "apple cart?" It may be that absolutely *no one else* wants to shoulder the various chores you've taken on.

You may be sick and tired of this grind or the commitments, but you were told that *you* are the only one to do it since no one else volunteered. Did you give in at that point, when it became uncomfortable, or did you write a letter of resignation, so to speak, giving them adequate notice to find someone else?

You might be surprised how quickly they would mobilize the other parents once they knew you were serious about stepping down! When they discover that attempting to manipulate you won't work, they will get very resourceful—guaranteed! And if they don't, it's *their* situation to resolve, isn't it? Yet, it will undoubtedly be at least somewhat uncomfortable.

So what'll help you keep your resolve through all the challenges? *SEEING* will help you move from just maintaining the status quo and maybe even backsliding in the quality of your life, to being uplifted by *SOARING* toward your dreams.

It'll probably still be at least a bit uncomfortable as you make your desires known, for example—to stop coaching or heading or participating on a particular committee. In fact your child(ren) may hassle you, trying to make you feel guilty for disappointing them. Let's face it, as soon as anyone "rocks the boat," *someone* is likely to be disappointed or angry to some degree. For one thing, no one can make you feel any particular way; it's up to you *how* you respond to their ploys. And also remember, as long as it doesn't actually harm someone else, what's good for you is good for everyone concerned, even though they might not understand it at the time.

SEEING helps to put the wind under your wings, so you can *SOAR* toward your dream. If you're not investing some time in your dream—that which you *really* want to be, do, and have—it isn't going to happen, pure and simple. No one else will do it *for* you. You're the key person. It's up to you whether you'll do whatever it takes to create the life you want.

Be solution-oriented! *SEE* what you want and look for ways to set aside the time in your schedule to make it happen. *SEEING* helps you to pause, catch your breath and be motivated enough to figure out what you need to do to create different results in certain areas of your life. *SEEING* helps you *believe* you *can* do it. *SEEING* is valuable for any area in which you want to make a change—not just to build your career or business and achieve your goals and dreams.

For example, let's say you want to change hairstylists. You are tired of traveling across town in rush hour traffic to the person who styled your hair when you lived in your old house. You have battled the traffic for six months and you don't want to *do* it anymore.

You *SEE* having an excellent hairstylist near your new home, making it convenient to stop by their salon on the way home from work. You picture yourself being happy with their hairstyling ability, prices, and personality. The next time you go for an appointment at the old place, you notice yourself feeling stressed as you go inside and complain about the traffic.

You had practiced *SEEING* your goal of making this change, even though you hadn't yet acted on it. When you're done getting your hair styled and anticipating agreeing to your old standing appointment, you start to feel uncomfortable. You now know you've about had it with this situation.

You courageously say to your hairstylist, "You've been doing a great job on my hair for all these years and I really appreciate you. However, since I've moved, it's really been time-consuming and stressful for me to drive across town every month to come here. Is there someone you could recommend who would be close to my new neighborhood?"

They may say, "Sure, call _____,"or, "I don't know anyone in that direction, but why don't you check with someone who lives in your neighborhood?" You are relieved, to say the least, that they make it that easy for you. But, even if they don't, you are still *SEEING* the new result you want. If their response is unpleasant and they *choose* to be offended, there's nothing you can do about it. After all, they don't own you as a customer.

Does this example help you understand how *SEEING* is an important part of getting what you want in life? It helps you stick to your convictions to make it—whatever that is for you—happen!

Since most people are busy these days, it helps to reassess what's really important to you. You need to set your own priorities. Perhaps you need to maintain some activities, juggle or delegate others, and eliminate those that no longer serve you and your dreams. This won't always be easy.

The clearer your vision *(SEEING)* is of your dream, the easier it will be for you to do what you need to do. You'll need to let go of some old habits and adopt some new ones to make the changes you want—whatever they may be for you. Be patient with the process. As former U.S. President Theodore Roosevelt once said, *"Do what you can, with what you have, where you are."* You *can* blast through any and all challenges you face and live your dream!

So practice *SEEING* and ask yourself, "Am I 'on-purpose' in my activities, or am I just avoiding potential disagreements with others whom I'm trying to please with my current choices?" Listen to what your heart tells you—rather than what your fears say!

Get out of your familiar zone. And, as you do the thing you fear, the fear will go away.

Whose Goals Are You Achieving Anyway?

First, if you have a job, you may be saying "I've got to do what my boss tells me to do." That may be true. And then it may only be true *some* of the time. Your boss may be open to other ideas, and you need to have the courage to share them. Have you ever considered that possibility, or have you been blindly pleasing them by immediate compliance to all their requests? Are you getting more and more frustrated as the days go by?

Do you find that, time and time again, you're really not getting what you want? If so, it may be because, until *now*, you haven't had *a big enough dream* to make it seem worthwhile for you to suggest other options. Could that be true? It's true for a lot of people in the formative stages of becoming committed to achieving their dreams.

SEEING your dream, *vividly and in detail*, helps you to follow your deepest convictions, regardless of other people's reactions.

Most people allow themselves to be pushed by their circumstances, rather than pulled by their dreams. As a result, their precious dreams are lost in the process. They *let* other people's (like their boss's) goals and dreams take precedence over their own. They're under the illusion that they can build their own dream someday, whenever they want to, and that it'll always be there.

How Solid Is the Vehicle You've Chosen?

Some people don't succeed like they could because they're investing themselves in the wrong vehicle, whether it's a job or a business. You need to choose a vehicle that'll give you what you're looking for.

You may want a vehicle you can participate in without affecting your current occupation. You may be looking for financial freedom. You may have noticed that very few people become wealthy working for someone else. So where does that lead you? Building your own business on the side could be the key for you. You can continue doing what you're doing at your job during the day or whenever it is you work. Outside of work, in your discretionary time, you could gradually build a business. That's how most successful people begin.

No matter what you choose to do, "the ball is in your court." And as the old saying goes, *"Actions speak louder than words."* What are you *doing* to make what you're *SEEING* a reality? Are you just passively waiting for your ship to come in? If you wait, guess what happens? Your dream waits too! Success isn't going to beat down your door—you need to make it happen.

It's like looking at a tree heavily loaded with ripened fruit: You can admire it from a distance, or you can take a few steps up and pluck at the sweetness dangling before you. Put another way, instead of waiting for your ship to come in, take the initiative and swim out to meet it! It's fun to ponder what life could be like if you decide to step right up and start taking charge of your success. Just step right up and claim what you are *SEEING*!

Back to Goals

Remember, you need to be sure that your goals are *your* goals and not someone else's! There is a great deal you can learn from role models, but you need to apply their teachings to your own life uniquely and individually. We've all been dealt a different "hand of cards" when it comes to looking at the talents, personalities, and emotions we possess. We all have obstacles to overcome along the road of success. To be successful, we need to set our dreams and goals according to who we are and what we want to be, do, and have...before we die. Success means different things to different people; it's very personal. What's *your* definition?

Mental Exercise

What Does Success Mean To You?

The Smart Money Says...

Ready for a huge momentum booster? Copy your dream on a piece of paper or "Post-It" type note and stick it up somewhere you'll see it every day. This may sound like an insignificant thing to do, but it's actually very powerful. In the course of a couple of minutes, you've taken a very important step toward becoming an achiever. You've chosen a path to pursue. The note on your mirror, or elsewhere, so you can see it every day will serve as a constant reminder to help you stay on course. This one simple act could prove to be a blockbuster in your efforts to SOAR!

Dream Big—*Yet Responsibly*

Because playing golf is not as important to me as it was earlier in my life when I played at the collegiate level, I've chosen to focus my dreams on things other than shooting sub-par rounds. I alluded to golf earlier in this chapter simply to illustrate a point regarding the unlimited boundaries you can approach, or exceed, in *SEEING*. It's important, however, to keep in mind the distinction between fantasies and serious dreams.

Your dreams parallel the things you truly desire out of life, while fantasies don't. I sometimes, just for the fun of it, fantasize about winning the U.S. Open, but I don't spend any time seriously dreaming about it. That's the primary difference between fantasizing and dreaming. Fantasies provide for a fun *escape*, but dreams are *more* fun because of their potential to come true and give you a different life.

Stretching yourself by reaching for worthwhile goals is what gives your life meaning and enjoyment. Remember how excited you felt the last time you accomplished that certain something you had always wanted to do? That certain something you weren't quite sure you could tackle at the outset? Those feelings of self-mastery and confidence raised you to new heights—you discovered that your potential was greater than you had originally imagined, right? It always is!

You'll never determine how far your potential stretches until you pick a point on the horizon and start SOARING toward it. We all have tremendous, untapped potential. The ultimate challenge in life is to live up to it. Discover what your potential is—and you'll discover who you really are. You'll find out what you can really do once you begin *SEEING* it.

Your future is yours for the *SEEING*. Remember the life-changing words of Preston Bradley—*"The world has a way of giving what is demanded of it. If you are frightened and look for failure and poverty, you will get them, no matter how hard you may try to succeed. Lack of faith in yourself, in what life will do for you, cuts you off from the good things of the world. Expect victory and you make victory. Nowhere is this truer than in business that is, where bravery and faith bring both material and spiritual rewards."*

Mental Exercise

Imagine It's the Year 2100

Looking through the contents of a 2×2×2 foot stainless steel box, the people in your hometown are sifting through information describing your life. What would you like them to discover?

What legacy do you want to leave behind to grow?

Chapter Summary

➤ Great achievements are accomplished by people who are courageous enough to *DREAM BIG!*

➤ Develop a passion for dreaming during your waking hours. Then, watch your confidence *SOAR* as you *SEE* yourself succeeding.

➤ Dreaming takes time and practice. Follow these simple guidelines:

1. Relax!
2. Establish a routine—put it in your date book or day planner.
3. Have fun!
4. Don't set limits.
5. Draw vivid mental pictures of your successes.
6. Put your dreams on paper
7. Hang pictures of your dreams where you'll see them every day.

➤ It's important that you develop a true understanding of yourself and know what you really want out of life. Once you've done this, you'll be more inclined to commit yourself to turning your dreams into realities. You *can* make it happen—lots of people have!

A Final Reflection on *SEEING*...

*If there were ever a time to
dare to make a difference, to do
something really worth doing, that
time is now. Not for any grand cause,
necessarily, but for something that tugs at
your heart, something that's your aspiration,
something that's your dream. You owe it to
yourself to make your days here count.
Have fun. Dig deep. Stretch.
Live your dream and
make a difference.*

Joyce Guila

*"I believe
very strongly
in the philosophy
of staying hungry.
If you have a dream
and it becomes a reality,
don't stay satisfied with it too
long. Make up a new dream
and hunt after that one
and turn it into reality.
When you have that
dream achieved,
make up a new
dream."*

Arnold Schwarzenegger

Chapter 5

ORGANIZING—YOU NEED TO HAVE A "FLIGHT" PLAN

"No one plans to fail; they fail to plan. So plan your work, then work your plan."
Author Unknown

ORGANIZING Is Key to Your Success

The *O* in *SOAR* stands for *ORGANIZING*, the second key to successful living. *ORGANIZING* gives you some of the wind beneath your wings that you need to *SOAR*. People who are consistently successful become so because they take the time to organize their dreams into a plan of action, with specific and measurable goals to achieve them.

Dreams of greatness in any career or business, or in any other arena for that matter, aren't realized by random, unfocused living. Such things hardly happen by accident, but rather by a joint effort of goal setting and plan development, coupled with on-purpose action.

Chiseling goals and plans out of dreams is not new at all. It's not something revolutionary, not a product of our new and improved age. And it's certainly not the creation of some individual whose brilliance is dwarfed only the number of degrees plastered on the wall!

The concept of *ORGANIZING* dreams into goals and action plans is, in fact, very straightforward. It has proven to be an essential ingredient in creating success for countless numbers of great men and women throughout history.

Success is achieved by following certain basic principles that don't require anyone to be a rocket scientist. Even so, most people still fail to commit the time and energy necessary to bring value to their goal setting exercises! How about you? The question I keep asking, again and again, is: "Why are people generally unwilling to put forth the required effort, overcome the obstacles, and make the necessary sacrifices to turn their grandest dreams into their greatest successes?" Nowhere is brilliance or strength or cunning factored into this simple question.

Let's talk about running a business, for example. All we're talking about here is effort. You need to invest some time developing a "flight" plan to duplicate the pattern of success that has already worked for innumerable other people. Then you need to consistently follow it toward your dreams.

I can't tell you how many times I've heard people say, "I would do anything if I could just...." But unfortunately, most people simple don't do anything—they won't devote any time to develop and work a plan that leads to their success. Then, amazingly, they blame others for their lack of achievement! Most people simply spend too much time looking for the shortcut—the so-called quick and easy approach—which inevitably winds up being more convoluted than the way that actually works. Following a proven plan *is* the shortcut! Poet Ella Wheeler Wilcox sums it up this way: *The fault of the age is a mad endeavor to leap to heights that were made to climb.* The people at the top didn't just suddenly arrive. They followed a proven flight plan.

Be Careful from Where and Whom You Get Information

As a person living in the Information Age, you are constantly bombarded with all kinds of information. You need to be careful of the sensationalistic, non-value-based, negative-attitude, purely entertainment-oriented things the media has to offer. This includes, but isn't limited to, information you can receive via the Internet, newspapers, television, movies, and advertisements.

As I've clearly and not so subtly stated, *ORGANIZING* a plan isn't rocket science, particularly when you consider all the valuable resources at your disposal. One of the great things about living in the Information Age, while building your career or business, is that there's a tremendous number of tools to educate, motivate, and encourage you. They can help you avoid the known pitfalls and succeed in getting where you want to go.

It's likely that you can periodically counsel with a leader or mentor in your career or business. Look for someone who's on track and where you want to be. This person can give you insight based on their knowledge and experience. Duplicate what they did to achieve their goals and dreams. They can recommend specific, positive personal development and educational books that can help you grow in key areas.

There may even be a continuing education program you can get on. Many companies realize how much this can help their people to make their businesses thrive. As you grow and become, you'll find yourself *SOARING* in your career or business, as well as in your personal life.

There may also be audio- and videotapes, as well as literature, that you can purchase. You can get up-to-the-minute taped information to build your career or business. Your leaders can point you in the right direction—they'll know what would help you excel.

There are also seminars and other activities to help you get and stay motivated as well as give you and your associates basic and leading-edge information. Check with your leader or mentor—they may have a schedule of events for when such activities are held. Put those dates into your day planner or date book so you can prepare to attend by lining up baby-sitters, adjusting your schedule, and the like.

Last of all, you may even be able to receive information via satellite or the Internet that will inspire and teach you how to grow yourself and enhance your career or business. The valuable information available to you is virtually endless and constantly expanding. Focus on positive, motivational, educational, personal, career, and business growth information. And be sure to let go of the "garbage" you get from the negative-thinking nay-sayers. Remember, *there are no statues erected to critics!*

If you're getting information from an unauthorized non-credible, non-expert source and feel you're being "negged-out", you need to decline it. You could have a disgruntled person who tried to do what you're intent on doing. They may be airing their complaints to you directly, through a friend, a family member, via the Internet, or elsewhere.

Their negative comments could just be a smokescreen for the real reason they didn't succeed—which they won't admit. Perhaps they never exerted the effort necessary to build their business or career. They're simply blaming others, or perhaps their circumstances, for their own lack of initiative. The truth is it's probably their own refusal to do whatever it takes that caused their failure.

Stay focused on information that's positive and growth inducing, that comes from those who are winning in the arena you have chosen. Associate with others who are doing what you want to do and are where you want to be.

Professionals and entrepreneurs who are really moving on in their careers or businesses don't listen to, or read, the negative news. Instead, they saturate their minds with positive, educational, motivational, and encouraging information. They replace years of often-negative input with positive information that *supports*, rather than undermines, their efforts to build their career or business. As the old adage says, *"A wise man will hear and increase learning, and a man of understanding will attain wise counsel."*

Standing on the Shoulders of Giants

As Sir Isaac Newton once said, *"We stand on the shoulders of giants."* By this, he meant that each generation learns from the collective knowledge of all previous generations. The knowledge of the ages is out there, waiting for you to retrieve it and apply it to your own life. You just need to duplicate the pattern of success already established by the experiences of already successful people. Use the system of career or business success appropriate for your vehicle, and follow the way of doing things to achieve the success you want.

When I started my first business, I began asking people who had successful businesses how they had begun. I checked out library books and took notes on entrepreneurs who had done the same thing. Finally, I took all of my collected information and *ORGANIZED* it into a plan I thought would work for me. Very little of it was Shawn Anderson original.

One secret to developing an effective plan of action, then, is really no secret at all! Just follow the lead of others whom you relate to and respect. Ask them to share their experiences with you so you're able to use their information in *ORGANIZING* your own plans. Counsel with your leader or mentor. They're doing whatever it takes, and using books, tapes, seminars, and attending career- or business-related activities.

Former U.S. President Abraham Lincoln didn't bring a divided nation together simply by wishing it so! He talked to people, rallied them around his cause, and organized his dreams into a detailed plan that guided his actions. You can do this too—on any scale, large or small.

To illustrate the importance of goal setting and planning, think in terms of the following metaphor: Life is like crossing your very own river (named after you, of course) with a strong, frothy current. Large stones cover some of your river's bed—jutting out, here and there, breaking the water's surface. Your big dream, which includes all of your small dreams, is found in crossing...

...Your River of Life

Your river is similar in some ways, but not identical to anyone else's. During your lifetime, you continually work toward the other bank so you'll have lived fully and prosperously—having accomplished your goals, and making your dream a reality. Even if you would win a lottery, you know you cannot go from one side of your river directly to the other. You need to carefully plot your way over the multitude of stepping stones—opportunities to grow—that span your river. Some view these stones as unwanted, but you know they're chances for you to learn, grow, and become—totally experiencing your uniqueness.

Immediately starting out by choosing a stepping stone to jump to, then another, then another—one rock at a time—isn't the best way to cross, either. You may wind up in the middle of the river before you realize you've chosen to cross in an area where the stones don't lead to where you want to go. Once again, it's like climbing the ladder of success, only to discover it's leaning against the wrong wall.

The best, and ultimately the quickest, way to cross the river is to choose a course of action from the safety of the bank you're on. Evaluate several paths across the river, then pick the one that looks like the best course for you. Keep in mind that the best path for you may not be the one everyone else chooses. After all, the beaten path is the rut most people, often unconsciously, choose. It's crowded, slow, and doesn't inspire or excite! It's boring!

Some of the stepping stones you encounter along the way are slippery, and you may stumble and get wet a few times. You are temporarily off course and need to regain your equilibrium. Even though you may slip and plunge into the cold water, you stay focused on your dream. You constantly picture your life on the other side of the river.

You've dreamed of success, and you have this exciting vision—the *SEEING* in *SOAR*—firmly planted in your mind through consistent practice. When you slip and fall into the water, you get out, dry off, and keep going. Eventually, with dogged perseverance, you reach the other side. For some of you that means you're being recognized, perhaps in front of your peers, for your accomplishments, telling your story, inspiring others.

Pictured in this light, you can see that *ORGANIZED* plans are the stepping stones to reaching your goals and dreams. To quote William Ellery Channing, *"All that a man does outwardly is but the expression and completion of his inward thought. To work effectively, he must think clearly; to act nobly, he must think nobly."*

Are You Really Focusing on Your Target?

On the surface, simply identifying your major goal—your dream—may seem like a fairly easy task. When I ask an audience to raise their hands if they have goals, everyone's hand usually goes up. They respond that they do indeed have goals by which they live their lives. And yet, when I ask people about specific goals in their lives, I find they typically lack the focus and passion that it takes to achieve them.

Mental Exercise

Ask Yourself the Following Questions:
➤ What steps do I need to take so I can achieve my dream?
➤ What hurdles are standing in my way that I need to overcome?
➤ How do I plan to overcome these hurdles?

These are the questions you need to ask yourself as you're choosing your goal, *SEEING* it, and *ORGANIZING* your action plan. When answered well, they can lead to a plan you can use to cross your metaphorical river and produce the results you want. When your mentor or leader learns that you're serious about building your career or business, they can be your strongest ally in helping you to map out a flight plan to do just that. Remember, *nobody plans to fail; they fail to plan.*

When Developing Plans—*Think Small to Make It BIG*

When you set your goals—think *BIG!* But when you develop your plans to achieve your goals, think small—

address all the little details. Both are equally important. Setting goals is useless without a plan to achieve them. In and of themselves, goals do absolutely nothing—zippo. A goal is simply a target for you to *SOAR* toward. To reach your target, the one you've been dreaming of, you need a plan. Man would never have gone to the moon had there not been a step-by-step plan developed to get from earth to their remote destination!

Let's pause and think about this for a moment...

Dateline 1962. The President of the U.S., John F. Kennedy, announced to the world that, within a decade, the U.S. would put a man on the moon. That's the equivalent of proclaiming today that within ten years we'll be doing lunch on Mars. Great, so we're going to Mars. Neat goal! There's nothing like thinking *BIG!*

Now what? How do we pull off this miraculous feat? Think of the hundreds of thousands of tasks that need to be completed before we could even begin to make this proposition a reality. Some of the things we will eventually need haven't even been invented yet! But, they'll be figured out along the way.

So Where Would You Begin in Your Quest to Reach Mars by Noon Ten Years from Today?

You'd get out of inertia by taking the first step. You'd develop your plan, beginning by simply outlining a few general ideas. This step doesn't require much more than filling in the blanks to the following sentence:

To Get to Mars (Or Whatever Your Goal Is), *I Need to Do the Following (or Whatever It Takes):*

1. Design and build a space ship.
2. Plot a course to Mars.
3. Choose the right astronauts.
4. You take it from here.

Next, in your quest to go to Mars, break down your tasks—tasks to which you can assign real people, real time frames, and deadlines. To build your spaceship, you're going to need to determine the parameters, design it, get materials, and find a place to manufacture and assemble the components. And to get materials for your spaceship, you'll need to review the designs for requirements, select vendors, and arrange for transportation and storage. In selecting vendors, you'll need to determine your budget, send out requests for proposals, review the requests, and so forth. Get the idea? Keep breaking bigger tasks down into smaller ones. Get into as much detail as possible. The more detailed your plans are, the better.

Say your dream is financial freedom. You may love your profession in the medical field or something else, but you want to be able to do it because it's your mission. Rather than having to get paid for doing it, you want to do it because you love it. You may want to open a charity clinic to serve the poor. You may need to get out of debt and create a residual income to do that. You may decide to *SOAR* in a business outside your profession, while, of course, still performing your responsibilities with integrity at your job or other business. So you'd potentially write:

To Gain Financial Freedom and Build My Clinic, *I Need to Do the Following.*

1 Get plugged into the pattern of success others have used to become successful.
2. Counsel regularly with my mentor or leader.
3. Develop a specific flight plan.
4. Work my plan until I reach my goals and get financially free.
5. Dream even bigger and repeat the process.
6. Build the clinic.

Every *BIG* dream can be broken down into doable action steps. You can achieve whatever dream is in your heart by planning your work and, day by day, working your plan. You can do it!

Let's continue the example of building your own business. You may not yet be sure of exactly what it is you want to do. You can get a general idea from this example and apply the ideas to your own situation.

Here goes...

Look again at the general plan you might have if you're dream is to become financially free. What would be the more specific actions you need to take? You'd need to block out some time in your day planner or date book to meet some people you could potentially associate with. After all, you can't be successful without the cooperation of other people.

You'd need to invest in a continuing education program of books, tapes, and seminars to learn more and keep yourself motivated. Then you could set aside the necessary funds to *invest* in yourself and your dream.

Being successful requires that you *plan* to be successful by duplicating the leaders in the industry you chose. Simply follow those who have already made it to the other side of the river where you want to be.

Did you notice that the seemingly impossible has just become possible? By accomplishing bits and pieces at a time, even the most challenging dreams are within your grasp. As some people say, *inch by inch, anything's a cinch.*

Sounds pretty simple, doesn't it? Well, it really is simple—challenging, but simple. And that's the way it works for the folks at NASA (the U.S. National Aeronautics and Space Administration) who plan "lunch dates with Martians," or, at least, with their fellow astronauts in space! That's also the way it works for someone like you—someone with a *BIG* dream.

The Four Faces of Inspiration

Another example that is a bit more down to earth, yet just as inspiring, is Mt. Rushmore in the U.S. According to Webster's New Universal Unabridged Dictionary, Mt. Rushmore is "a peak in the Black Hills of South Dakota that is a memorial having 60-foot (18-meter) busts of former U.S. Presidents Washington, Jefferson, Lincoln, and Theodore Roosevelt..." Until the day my wife and I stood below this tribute to American greatness, I never knew just how tremendous an undertaking creating this monument was. The drilling on this massive mountain of granite began in 1927. Work continued until 1941 when the finishing touches were applied.

Carving the gigantic faces of the four Presidents must have seemed like an impossible project, especially in 1927! In the beginning Mt. Rushmore sculptor Gutzon Borglum's inventory list must have read something like this:

Mt. Rushmore Project
Inventory List

> A BIG dream.
> One drill.
> One towering solid expressionless land mass.
> Miscellaneous ropes and platforms.
> One box of dynamite.

Picture this—someone walks up to you, points to the side of a huge granite mountain, and says, "I'm going to transform that mountain into the faces of four great men." How would you respond? What could you possibly say to encourage someone to undertake a project of that magnitude? Think of it another way—picture a mountain with which you are familiar. Now picture yourself doing your best to carve faces into the mountainside. Where would you begin? Sure, at the beginning. But where's that?

The trick, as Borglum discovered, is to tackle the mountain one face at a time. In the time it took to make that simple decision, the project mentally became about one quarter as difficult as it was previously. As Henry Ford once said, *"Nothing is particularly hard if you divide it into small jobs."* The great task of chiseling even one face was broken down into smaller phases, like creating the nose and the eyes. Still smaller tasks, like creating the pupil and the eyelids were planned until, finally, the job seemed workable.

The same holds true for your individual goals. Take the time to figure out the steps necessary to achieve your dreams, and then break these steps down into smaller steps that become easier and easier to accomplish. Voila! You've organized your dreams into a well-thought-out plan of action. As you take these small steps in rapid succession, you find yourself racing across that metaphorical river and *SOARING* toward the attainment of your dream.

By following the principle of *O* in *SOAR*, and *ORGANIZING* your dreams into goals and specific plans, you're on your way to being successful. But to make sure you arrive at your destination somewhere close to your ETA (Estimated Time of Arrival), you also need to do more than simply know the way. To avoid making too many "landings" that impede your progress, you need to know when you plan to arrive at your destination.

To be successful in anything, you need to *ORGANIZE* yourself to do different things. If you simply continue doing what you've always done, you'll continue getting what you've always gotten. For example, if you decided to buy a franchise, you'd need to rent or buy a building and some land. You'd also buy or lease equipment, pay the franchise fee(s), hire people to run it, and so on. You simply have to do different things to get different results.

The same principle of *ORGANIZING* is true for building a strong, growing career or business. You need to *ORGANIZE* your life to accommodate your career or business activities. Plan to do something every day toward the realization of what you're *SEEING*.

ORGANIZE your plans.

Keeping Your Dreams Alive with Deadlines

Deadlines help you to stay on track and help you avoid the godfather of all dreamstealers—procrastination! The size of your goals and dreams, and the breadth of your plans, will determine how many deadlines you'll need to set. As I develop my own personal flight plans, I set deadlines and then work backward from the deadline dates to the present date, determining what needs to be done and by when.

A good example was my preparation for running my first marathon.

I was strictly a recreational runner when, during my senior year of college, I decided to run a marathon. It sounded like an enormous undertaking—running 26 miles without stopping—and I wanted to learn if I could do it. After all, lots of other people do it, so why couldn't I?

Little did I know that leaving the three-day-a-week leisure crowd to join the world of big league marathoning would be so incredibly challenging!

Now that I had this goal, I needed to *ORGANIZE* my plan of attack. There were a couple of steps I knew I needed to take before I even placed one Nike-clad foot onto the pavement to begin training for this 26-mile endeavor. Primarily, I needed to put myself in a position to win—where I could realistically accomplish the Feat of Feets.

The Smart Money Says...

Bring a lot of "carrots" with you when you decide to tackle a big project. Carrots are little indulgences that you enjoy along the way. Tie these personal treats to the completion of tedious tasks. Rewards like this are good for your eyesight—they help you to see and focus on the light at the end of the tunnel.

An example of this could be to add a day or two of vacation onto an out-of-town business trip or activity. You could enjoy golfing, boating, visiting the tourist sites, going to the beach, or something else. Check with your mentor/leader to determine what they recommend. Be sure it fits in with your financial and time situation.

Mental Fitness First

First, I addressed the mental aspect. I knew training for a marathon would be a long, hard, exhausting experience. I knew it would be a big challenge for me to continue motivating myself—day in and day out—and continue putting in the miles of road work necessary to build up my endurance.

But my dream was big and I was determined. So I asked my friend and recreational running partner, Danny, to join me in this quest. As the saying goes, *"Teamwork makes the dream work."* We figured we could help each other stay motivated during the long weeks of training by challenging each other during practice sessions. We pushed each other to continue moving forward, and our training sessions became mini-competitions. These helped give us a sorely needed shot of adrenaline during the middle part of our training period.

Motivation is generally easier at the beginning and end of a goal achievement process. There's plenty of excitement involved in starting or finishing something. It's that period in the middle that you need to be concerned about. It's when the newness has worn off and "the light at the end of the tunnel" isn't yet in sight. This is when you'll especially need to work on staying enthusiastically focused on your dream in order to keep yourself going. It's this middle ground that tests your commitment.

Motivation, like adrenaline, tends to work in short spurts. It's like a bath or shower—you need it every day—it simply doesn't last. This is why it's so important to have a self-responsibility system—associates, deadlines, prioritized task lists, personal journals, coaches, mentors, leaders, and the like—to keep you accountable and on track. Another key is to be dedicated to continuous improvement. Listening to tapes and reading daily from a positive book are keys to your growth. Attend seminars regularly, as it's so beneficial to associate with other positive thinkers and doers. All this helps you to continually re-ignite your fire so you can blast through the obstacles more easily.

Getting back to the marathon example—next, Danny and I set deadlines. First, we decided to tackle the California International Marathon which was to be held in Sacramento—just two months from the date we committed to this goal! Now we had established where we wanted to be and when we wanted to get there. All that remained was to figure out how to get to our destination 26 miles down the road. For this we needed to *ORGANIZE* a training plan.

Working Backward—*to Move Forward*
Knowing that we needed to be able to run 26 consecutive miles, we prescribed a workout schedule for ourselves. Like best-selling author Stephen R. Covey says, *"Begin with the end in mind."* So starting from the day before the race and *working backward* to the present day, we calculated the number of days we'd run each week. We also determined the benchmark distances we needed to achieve by the end of each week, so we'd be able to run the whole 26 miles by the end of the ten-week practice period.

This *ORGANIZED* workout schedule served two purposes. First, it assured us that we'd be physically prepared for the race. Second, it helped us to hold ourselves accountable for following through with the crazy idea.

When the day of the marathon finally arrived, both Danny and I had completed several 20-mile practice runs and felt no worse for the wear. But the race would be 26 miles long, and that still seemed a bit overwhelming. We needed another plan—a mental plan—to help get us over the hump and propel us toward the finish line.

"Bite-Sized" Focus Makes a Meal of Big Goals and Dreams

To complete the race, *we decided to break down the course into a series of five-mile increments.* At the beginning of the race, we focused on finishing the first five miles. At the completion of the fifth mile, we wiped our mental slates clean and *focused only on making it to the tenth mile*—nothing more. Our strategy: We knew that when we successfully completed each of the five-mile stages, we'd be getting closer and closer to our big goal and eventually wind up at the finish line. By focusing on bite-sized chunks of mileage, we knew we could finish the race.

As we persisted, the 26 miles was gradually reduced to 21 miles, then 16 miles, and so on. By the time we got beyond the last five-mile chunk, we'd have only one mile to go!

Get with your leader or mentor and create a progressive series of short-term plans and goals that lead to your long-term goal—your dream. The *ORGANIZED* plan helps you concentrate all of your efforts on accomplishing what you believe is attainable. By continuing to strive for the attainable and putting one foot in front of the other, what now seems unattainable will take care of itself.

We kept persevering, focusing on the bite-sized five-mile chunks. And yes, we did manage to finish the marathon. All the *ORGANIZED* planning, goal setting, and effort paid off!

I was absolutely elated when we reached the finish line, incredibly fired-up that I did what I had set out to do. Words don't do justice to explain how victorious I felt. As exhausted as I was, I had a sense of inner strength and self-mastery because I accomplished something that, at the start, I wasn't sure I could do. And it all happened one step at a time.

All the goals you set for yourself in your own life can be broken down in a similar fashion. I refer to this as the "Just

Make It to the Next Mile" goal-setting plan. The strength of this plan is that it holds you accountable and keeps you focused and *SOARING*.

Accountability—*The Stuff Real Plans Are Made Of*

As I've mentioned, accountability is the real cornerstone of success. An accountability, or self-responsibility, system keeps you on course. *If you don't build accountability into your plans, all of your planning is for naught.*

Sticking to this marathon example, let's suppose you've broken your own quest down into "next mile" stages. You've mapped out your highway to the stars, and you've identified your stepping stones. You have a plan of attack. But will you ever get there? Eventually. *Maybe.*

But just getting there isn't enough. You don't want to spend the rest of your life running just one race, right? You want to finish one race and move on to the next. Although it's important, it's not enough to *just* break your journey down into "next mile" stages. You need to determine, with the help of your leader or mentor, how long you intend to invest time in completing each stage.

Notice I said *invest*. When you devote time to building your business or career, you're investing your time in your financial future, rather than just "spending" time.

If you watch situation comedy (sitcom) television rather than working on your dream, you're just whiling away your time—*that's* spending (wasting) time. When you *invest* time, you are receiving some sort of return—personal development, monetary, making a difference, or the like. *Entrepreneurial thinking is investment thinking*, versus just frittering away time. This is appropriate no matter what your vehicle is.

Your goal achievement deadline is your accountability. This is your gauge to let you know how you're progressing.

Are you doing whatever it takes? Are you ahead of schedule? Are you behind? If you're behind, how much do you need to speed up to stay within your original time frame? Do you need to do more?

When you're flying high, counsel with your leader or mentor for guidance on how to keep it up. Perhaps you've underestimated your ability to make it happen. We're all capable of doing more than we thought we could.

In essence, these are *your* deadlines. And once again I stress their importance as a part of this *ORGANIZING* formula.

Ask your leader or mentor to help you set some goals for your business or career. When do you want to be at your next level of accomplishment? Your leader or mentor can help you map out a flight plan so you can achieve your goals and dreams.

When you show your leader or mentor, through taking consistent action, that you're doing whatever it takes to make it happen, they're more likely to be willing to help you. They'll know you're serious—that you're committed—and walking the walk, instead of just talking the talk, like so many people do.

Be diligent about following a proven pattern of success one day at a time, and you can, inch by inch, reach your goals one by one. Be sure to enjoy the process. After all, as the saying goes, *"Success is a journey, not a destination!"*

The Smart Money Says...

When determining deadlines for each segment of your action plan, remember to factor in some slack time to compensate for unforeseen circumstances and delays. However, do set goals that cause you to stretch. Then stick to them!

Truly impossible deadlines are almost as detrimental to long-term achievement as having no goals at all. Miss a few tight deadlines and your morale will inevitably start diminishing. This is the quickest way I know to turn lofty plans and dreams into aborted takeoffs. Challenge yourself to fly higher than ever before, but don't take foolish chances. Give yourself an honest chance to reach your goals. Once again, your leader or mentor can help you with this.

Simple Plans Can Help You Yield—*Powerful Results!*

I mentioned earlier that I challenged some people to elaborate on the goals they said they had set. Sadly, I found that most of them lacked a plan of action. Even though every single one of them had a goal, most had no idea how to make them happen and no time frames in which to accomplish them.

Plans bring strength. Simple, straightforward plans are *key* to *your* success. Plans are the steel girders that support your goals and dreams. Plans keep them together in the midst of storms of distractions and unexpected occurrences. That, coupled with your dreams, makes your life, shall we say, interesting. In fact, sometimes it's just downright amazing what can happen when you challenge your resolve.

Plans give you clarity. Have you heard people saying, "I'll do it someday?" How about you? Have you ever said that? *Someday* is a non-committal term, to put it mildly! Someday turns into never and spells the death of a dream. *Don't let your dream die!*

When you plan, you pull yourself out of vague fogginess—the mental state most people seem to be in. When you're committed to achieving your dream, you become keenly aware of the actions you need to take and what your time line is. In the process, you gain clarity. This is a key to making your dream a reality rather than always yearning for it, but never doing whatever it takes to make it happen. As you gain clarity, you'll know in your heart that you can do it.

Plans are empowering. Simple, organized plans, as uncomplicated as they are, can generate an incredible amount of passion in your life. The more time you invest thinking about and developing your plans for success, the more convinced you will be that your actions will result in realities. At the other end of the spectrum again, you need to move from planning to action rather than getting stuck in analysis, which we'll talk about in the next chapter.

The more conviction you have, the more committed you become to following through on your own plan to achieve your dream. You're mentally *claiming your success*. Remember, it's your degree of commitment and devotion that truly measures your probability of success. These qualities are essential to support you in taking consistent action, regardless of the challenges you need to overcome along the way.

Soon after achieving your first few milestones along your path of success, you begin to build up a *momentum of self-confidence* that feeds on itself. After committing yourself to your plan of attack, you begin to see just how readily success can be attained. You feel good about yourself and your likelihood of achieving success. You begin committing more time and making an even *greater* effort to accomplish your goal. Soon, people begin to sit up and take notice as you ascend, *SOARING* toward success!

When you're consistently taking action, based on your plan, it starts happening. Everything just seems to fall into place. And it all begins with a simple, straightforward plan of action. Nothing fancy. Nothing that takes an engineering degree to decipher. Just a series of tasks that you can accomplish—one after another after another after another. In the end, you'll wind up carving your own personal Mt. Rushmore. You'll bring your dream to life. And some people will wonder how you could have possibly achieved it! While they're still trying to figure that out, you're busy dreaming even bigger dreams and creating your next plan!

Do you honestly want to *SOAR*? If so, *ORGANIZING* your goals into specific plans is absolutely essential! Decide now to give your goals strength, clarity, power, and passion! Invest the time and effort to develop a simple, organized plan that, when followed, will be the key to your turning your dreams into reality!

Mental Exercise

What Lifetime Goals Have You Established and What Do You Need to Do to Achieve Them?

Use a blank sheet of paper to list all of your lifetime goals; we list a few suggestions below to get you started. Next to each goal, outline the steps needed to achieve these goals.

1. Family
2. Fitness/Health
3. Continuing Education/Skill Development
4. Career/Business
5. Financial
6. Spiritual
7. Personal Development/Habits/Attitudes
8. Friends
9. Community Involvement/Charities You Want to Support
10. Travel

Chapter Summary

➤ People who are consistently successful become so because they take the time to *ORGANIZE* their dreams into specific and measurable goals.

➤ To cross your river, you need to evaluate the best direction to go and then jump, one rock at a time.

➤ When you develop a simple, organized plan to achieve your goals, your purpose and passion are multiplied.

➤ To tackle the mountain as Gutzon Borglum did, you need to do it one face at a time. One nose at a time. One detail at a time.

➤ By setting and sticking to deadlines, while striving to achieve your goals, you dramatically increase your likelihood for success.

➤ The seemingly unattainable can be accomplished by taking the "Just Make It to the Next Mile" approach.

Final Reflections on *ORGANIZING...*

"The tragedy of life doesn't lie in
not reaching your goal. The tragedy lies in
having no goal to reach for. It isn't a calamity to die
with dreams unfulfilled, but it is a calamity not to dream.
It is not a disgrace not to reach the stars, but it is
a disgrace to have no stars to reach for.
Not failure, but low aim, is a sin."

Benjamin Mays

"Destiny is not a matter of chance, it is
a matter of choice: it is not a thing to be waited for,
it is a thing to be achieved."

William Jennings Bryan

"This is true joy of life—
the being used for a purpose that is recognized
by yourself as a mighty one instead of being a feverish, self-
ish little clod of ailments and grievances,
complaining that the world will not devote
itself to making you happy."

George Bernard Shaw

"Your thoughts control your life."

Robert Stuber

"I simply can't think of sleep. I have an ocean yet to cross and Paris to find.... Sleep can come later after I land."

Charles Lindbergh

Chapter 6

ACTING—MAKING THINGS HAPPEN IS KEY TO YOUR SUCCESS!

*"The man who does things makes mistakes,
but he who doesn't makes the biggest
mistake of all—doing nothing."*
Benjamin Franklin

Taking the First Step

In the previous chapter, I described goal setting in terms of running a marathon. Any long journey begins with a single step; however, you'll never make it to the finish line if you don't take that first step across the starting line! Having the courage to take that first step is the beginning of all success. You can have an admirable goal, and a great plan of attack, but they don't mean a thing unless you *act* on them!

The third letter in *SOAR* is *A* for *ACTING*. This is the dynamic principle that separates the winners from the wannabes, the movers from the moaners. By *ACTING*, you begin accomplishing the things you planned to do in order to reach your dream. You move yourself off "square one," where most people live with their "song" forever unsung. They die with their "music" still in them. And they often lead lives of not so quiet desperation.

You can carefully plan your steps across the proverbial river, but until you begin using your feet and taking steps, you haven't gotten anywhere! Even the best plans in the world are absolutely worthless—unless, of course, they're acted upon. After all, as the old sayings go, *"Talk is cheap,"* and *"Actions speak louder than words!"*

Some people are so busy just *thinking* about building their business or career that they tire themselves out! They go to seminars and other business-related activities; they listen to tapes; they read the recommended books—yet they never even reach a meaningful level of success in their industry!

How come? They never take the first step of putting what they've learning into action. Or, perhaps, they started *ACTING* but stopped as soon as they got a no from someone or encountered another obstacle. Maybe they're in the habit of quitting on themselves when they discover that being successful is basically simple, but not easy. They may not realize that overcoming the challenges is an essential part of all success, small or large. Those unwilling to do so often lead a life of just making a living rather than creating a life.

If any of this rings true for you, you can make that choice to get out of the rut you may be in. Take that first step and then keep on going step by step toward your dream, until it's yours. Just consider all your past mistakes and failures as valuable learning experiences. They're all a part of what has brought you here, to this moment, so you can really start to *SOAR* and make things happen.

In their book *In Search of Excellence*, Thomas J. Peters and Robert H. Waterman, Jr. spent years identifying eight basic principles that helped the best-run American companies stay on top. The first factor they noted was a bias for action. This is simply a preference for doing something—anything—rather than sending a question through cycles and cycles of analyses and committee reports.

Paralysis of Analysis

Let's take a close look at the "paralysis of analysis." A good example of it involves a conversation I had with a friend whom I'll call John. He worked for a high-profile international company. One day, in conversation with me, John described his proposal for a publishing department. He explained how it could save the company hundreds of thousands of dollars every year.

He described the volumes of reports and studies he was asked to produce for a carousel of committees involved in the project's final approval. Understandably, John, a go-out-and-get-'em kind of guy, was frustrated and suffocated in a bureaucracy that suffered from an acute case of paralysis of analysis. After he spent two years working, waiting, politicking, and then working and waiting some more, John told me most of his energy and enthusiasm for the project had dissipated.

Eventually, his idea was approved and, despite being one-fifth the size John originally envisioned, saved his company about $350,000 in its first year of operation. Imagine the opportunities and savings John's company missed out on over the two years it spent deliberating on, instead of acting upon, this project.

Ideas Alone Aren't Enough...

John's story is far from an isolated example of paralysis of analysis! There have been many great business plans developed by countless companies and individuals that we've never even heard about! The reason? There was never any action taken to follow through with these plans to make them a reality. The agenda of maintaining the status quo won out. Great ideas are a dime a dozen. It seems everybody has their own notion of what will bring in new business, what will work, and what is needed. Many of these ideas are genuinely good ones, too! But ideas, by themselves, don't bring in new business or guarantee success. Ideas themselves don't make money, and ideas alone never accomplish what needs to be done to succeed. *ACTION*, however, does!

When you set about doing something—whatever it may be—you're separating yourself from the enormous huddle of armchair quarterbacks. They simply sit back and lob sure-fire ideas from the comfortable vantage point of their favorite reclining television-watching chair or couch!

Former U.S. President Franklin Roosevelt, once said, *"We have always held to the hope, the belief, the conviction that there is a better life, a better world, beyond the horizon."* There is a lot of obvious truth to this. Then, how come you're in the minority when you're working diligently to achieve your dreams? What's the reason most people aren't "hungry" enough to work hard, let alone work smart? How come you stand out in the crowd when you operate with honesty and integrity? When you stand for something honorable, and commit to it? Why is it that such a minority participate as entrepreneurs in a free enterprise system or excel significantly in their jobs?

Amazingly, when you just go out and do something and work hard and smart at it, you'll be in the league of achievers who represent only a small fraction of the world's population! Commit yourself to pushing forward and following through on your promises and plans. Take appropriate action, and you'll begin to *SOAR* above the crowd.

As former President of the U.S. Harry Truman once said: *"I found that the men and women who got to the top were those who did the jobs they had in hand, with everything they had of energy and enthusiasm and hard work."*

It sounds so easy! So what's the catch? Why isn't everybody doing it? Three little words: *lack of commitment.*

Procrastination—*The Dream Deflator*

Think about how many times you've wound up in front of the television, watching something with little meaning to you, knowing there was something else you had planned to do, but didn't. Why? Have you ever thought about that? Simply put, we've all succumbed to that monster known as procrastination. We've all put off something important—something we needed to do—for something we could do passively. It was probably done without any thought to speak of, since it was just an old habit.

Have you noticed how easy it is to continually create small projects in order to rationalize putting off more important, and more challenging, tasks? To get where you want to be in life takes time and effort—*"legwork" is definitely required.*

Sure, it's easier to put off the tough stuff until tomorrow. But keep this in mind—the blocks to your house of success are laid one at a time. The time it takes you to reach the top floor is largely up to you. However, the more diligent you are at doing whatever it takes, and the stronger your commitment, the more likely you are to make it. Failed New Year's resolutions, notorious for their high concentration of noble intentions, are perfect examples of what happens when commitment is non-existent or weakens.

Even the best-conditioned achievers can grow weary from carrying out tedious and unglamorous tasks, if they allow their commitment to wane. Some of the events that are most important in moving us ahead and achieving success are downright dull. Most people put them off until "one of these days," which turns into "none of these days!"

Failing to do the tough stuff and falling victim to procrastination are sure tickets to failure. Watch out and be aware of your actions. The power to make and keep commitments with yourself is essential to your being effective. How can you honestly expect to stop procrastinating if you're not even committed to your *own* dream?

When you're firmly committed to persisting until you reach one goal after another, *your commitment wins out over the tendency to procrastinate.* Your commitment is so strong—such a driving force—that it overrides any old habits of procrastination which previously kept you stuck.

While you're *SOARING*, your wings may start to feel the "downdraft" of procrastination. You may lose some altitude, but your commitment will keep you going until you find more lift and start *SOARING* once again.

Mental Exercise

Become Aware of the Times When You Procrastinate.

Think of a recent time where procrastination won out and you failed to do something you wanted to do.

The Blocks in the Middle Are the Heaviest...

The toughest part of building your house of success isn't laying the first few building blocks in place. The initial surge of excitement you feel when starting something new makes short order of this work. It isn't applying the finishing touches either—that's always fun! The most challenging part of building your house of success is stacking all those middle blocks that lead from the foundation to the peak of the roof.

These blocks, the middle blocks, need to be carefully laid, one after another, in seemingly endless succession. It is when you are lining up these blocks that there oftentimes seems to be no end in sight. It is here where you need *persistence*.

Building your personal house of success is very similar to building a block wall. As you keep putting the blocks in place, your muscles begin to ache. The blocks start feeling heavier. The novelty of your new endeavor has worn off. It doesn't seem to be as much fun as it was when you were just getting started.

You've worked both hard and smart, and you gave it your all. And yet, when you step back and take a look at your progress, all you see are blocks arranged in a rough outline. The big picture hasn't begun taking shape yet, and the rewards for putting these middle blocks in place are usually not immediate.

You may have had to win out over your old habit of wanting immediate gratification. You know that building your business or career—your house of success—requires delayed gratification. But, gee, how long do you need to wait?

A lot of your old friends while away their time watching television or sipping lemonade sitting in the shade. If such a temptation strikes you, just remind yourself how much they complain. Ask yourself, "Do I really want to be where they are?" You know too much to say yes. The business or career you dreamed of building may look far from complete. But you can plug yourself into your industry's system of success even deeper to stop your enthusiasm from waning.

You hang onto your dream and call for support from the person who's helping you. They take you dreambuilding. You have a delicious lunch together under a sun umbrella on the patio of a beautiful open-air restaurant. You feel refreshed and encouraged. It's sure great to get some encouragement.

With your commitment strengthened, you return to building your house of success. You muster up your willpower and push yourself out the door to get productive. You meet some new potential business associates or customers. You talk to a group or meet with someone one-on-one, or you're doing something else to achieve your goal.

You're staying committed and accepting no excuses from yourself. You've got it that it's no one else's job to make you successful. The ball is in your court and you know it. You also know that—*starting is half-done.*

The Smart Money Says...

Get recharged when you need to, and then keep on going!

Achievers are people who stick with the ACT NOW principle and effectively manage their activities to accomplish what's most important every day. They are proactive versus reactive. They realize they're responsible for their lives and make value-based choices through initiative. They're clearly in charge of their activities.

Only with proactivity is there lasting success and long-term fulfillment. Even millionaires have only 24 hours a day. Think about it! They simply use their 24 hours more effectively and, as a result, get more important things done. That's how they get ahead. They "plus out" their time, as much as possible, with activities that move them closer to their goals.

The "Voices" of New Year's Resolutions Past

If you've ever made a New Year's resolution, you know how easy it is to lose sight of your goals. It's one thing to set a goal, but it's something else altogether to follow through with the diligent effort it takes to achieve it. There seems to be this little voice in the back of our minds, some mutant gene in our mental chemistry, that whispers to us, "Stop. You don't really have to go to all this trouble. So you're a couple of pounds overweight—so what? Is that such a terrible thing? Should you really have to deprive yourself of that box of chocolates lying open on the counter over there? Oh, go on—just take one. Or two, maybe. Yeah, that's it…you deserve a break…"

Sound familiar? Of course, once we've strayed from our commitment—even if we only took *one* of the chocolates and suddenly developed an ironclad willpower that refused the second—it becomes easier and easier to stray from our chosen path in the future.

In life, there are a lot of counter tops with little pieces of chocolate on them. And once you relinquish control to the little voice—even once—you'll find it getting louder and louder until you pay attention to it. Pretty soon you're listening to that mutant gene without hesitation. The light at the end of the tunnel begins to fade, and the dream dies. We end up missing out on an opportunity to do something we really had our hearts set on from the outset. The great thing is, *today is the first day of the rest of your life.* Your tomorrows can be different than your yesterdays. It's all up to you.

What can you do? You can adopt a few simple rules...

How To Be an *"Act Now"* Person...

...and accomplish your dreams!

1. Keep Pulling the Trigger!

To be an "act now" person, you must first have to want to be one! You need to develop a mind set that's automatically triggered to perform. When the thought of doing something important to your plan of action first comes into your mind—bang!—you condition yourself to do it. You pull the trigger!

2. Work During "High Tide!"

Get to know yourself. During which hours of the day are you most productive? Investing your time most effectively means working when you feel "hot!" When do you feel most creative? Most energetic? Everyone has a different internal clock, and discovering when your peak productivity hours are may take some experimentation. Taking charge and getting active in the pursuit of your goals and dreams is easier when your energy levels—mental, physical, emotional—are at high tide.

You may discover that your natural high tide is in the morning. But what if you're working at your job in the morning and not able to do things in the pursuit of new levels in your career or business? You could ask yourself, "How can I make the most of this energy?" Perhaps you could meet a prospect, customer, or business associate for breakfast at a local restaurant. It's a good way to start the day.

Now, you may ask, "What about my energy level later in the day? What can I do to boost it to maximize my effectiveness after work, when it's my time to shine for me?"

Discover what gets you super-charged! Is it the continuing education tapes you listen to? Are you taking full advantage of the great tool a tape is? Are you playing them as you get ready for work, before you go to bed, and in your car on your commute back and forth to work? Even if you're car pooling, walking, or taking a bus, you can use a portable audio cassette player with earphones, as long as you're not driving. These tapes are a key to your level of motivation and skill.

Of course, as exciting as these tapes are, you need to take action too! You're only fooling yourself if you don't. But the point here is that you can shift your energy into high tide when you need to.

How about playing some music that gets you super-charged? If you attend large business-related functions, there's often a band playing at certain points, perhaps between speakers. It's likely that the band has a back-of-the-room table where tapes are available. It's in your best interest to purchase such tapes. They can help you to create your own high tide.

3. Avoid "Dormancy Dungeons"!

People are creatures of habit, and it's easy to slip into a routine. For example, some people come home from a hard day's work and prop their feet up on the coffee table in front of the television and watch the predominantly negative news.

Learn to eliminate such non-productive activities during times you've set aside for achievement. Avoid situations that can be a distraction from the thing you need to do to be moving toward your goals and dreams.

Say you need to make some phone calls to prospects because your goal is to make ten presentations each week. So far, you've only booked five appointments. And since you know some may cancel out, you realize you need to set up more appointments than you'd like to do *to meet your goal.*

To get yourself super-charged, you take a 20-minute brisk walk and a quick shower, all while you're listening to a tape you love. You've made the breakthrough to get yourself in motion toward building your house of success rather than watch the reporters on television make money. You've broken free of being trapped in a dormancy dungeon. Isn't it great?

Rather than getting lured into dormancy dungeons and then looking for an escape route a bit later, avoid them altogether. Making the most of your life means making the most of your time, every day.

4. Divide and Conquer!

Sometimes you need a few little successes to get your confidence up and get you going in the right direction. If something seems unmanageable, too complex, or intimidating, break it down into smaller steps. Then start picking these activities off one-by-one—like tin cans at a shooting gallery. As the cans fall, your confidence will begin to *SOAR!*

For example, say you're preparing to make a presentation. You're meeting with some important people and you're a little nervous. You need to do one small thing first. So you bravely stand up, and begin giving the first part of your presentation to your dog or cat as your audience! Then you do the next part, and so on. Before you know it, you've made the whole presentation!

5. Write Now!

One of the surest ways to guarantee that you finish what you've planned for on a given day is to write it down and give it a priority. With a list of prioritized tasks in front of you, you have an accountability system for yourself. Think of this list as a challenge; you owe it to yourself to finish everything on it.

Leaders often use day planners or seven-day organizers like those produced by Franklin/Covey. Carry the planner/organizer with you everywhere you go during the day. Use it to keep track of your progress. Discipline yourself, and jot down the ideas you want to remember.

Ask your mentor or leader for a schedule of seminars, and other continuing education and motivational activities they might recommend for your growth. Put these things into your planner/organizer right away. Carrying this constant reminder with you helps keep you aware of your priorities all day, every day. It'll tell you when you need to reschedule an activity or perhaps renegotiate a prior commitment because of your new priorities. When it's in your planner/organizer, staring you right in the face, you're reminded of what you need to do to be successful.

6. Stop Making Excuses!

Refuse to accept a "reason"—an excuse—not to do what you need to do to be successful. An excuse can be defined as *a thin shell of truth stuffed with a lie, a ruse, or a cover-up!* Once you've committed to your success and eliminated the option to give up on yourself, you'll be amazed at how easily you're able to turn obstacles into opportunities. Keep telling yourself that *failure is not an option. There's no excuse not to be successful.*

7. Create Competition for Yourself!

While jogging halfway through a two-mile course up a mountain near my home, I feel the muscles in my legs tighten, and I start gasping for air. Thinking about making it to the top of this mountain becomes tough when it's all I can do to take another step. I've "hit the wall," and I need help to get over the top.

At points like these, I find myself occasionally thinking back to high-school days—I remember how easy it was to stay in shape during basketball season. I can hear the echo of a whistle and the pounding of 14 pairs of sneakers as, stopwatch in hand, our coach "encouraged" us to run faster in our drills ("C'mon, you bunch of prima donnas. Move your rears!" was the way he phrased it). The fastest I ever ran in my life were the times I diligently strove to avoid being the trailer—the guy the coach would "chew-on" the most.

Looking back, I marvel at how easy it seemed. Why? I was empowered by the "super nova" of energy known as *competition.* It made it a thousand times easier to push myself to new heights and be motivated to exceed what I believed were my upper limits. Endeavoring to beat 13 other guys and avoid the coach's wrath was exhilarating. All the motivation I ever needed was built right into the system.

Now, as I struggle midway through my run up the mountain, all I have to do is look over my shoulder to see my wife, pushing just as hard, right beside me. It's awfully hard to stop when I know she won't! I exercise with my wife as much as possible because then I'm certain to put in a good effort.

The Smart Money Says...

Getting things done is always easier when you have someone else holding you accountable. I dare you to ask your mentor/leader to be that someone else!

The Smart Money Also Says...

Compete against yourself by doing things better and faster than you ever did before. Also, keep track of your improvements by writing down your results.

In business, as well as in life, the competition is *really* with yourself. It's not about whether you can beat the other guy or gal—all that does is get you into a comparison mode which can devastate your self-esteem (the respect you feel for yourself). There will almost always be people who'll do better than you and those who'll do worse! Look to leaders in your industry, who are where you want to be, as your examples.

There will probably be at least one person you relate to the most, who might well have been in a career or business like yours at one time. Someone who "took the ball and ran with it." Someone who *SOARED* from one level to the next. Someone who is an example of being teachable, humble, and a student of the pattern of success established by those who won big in your industry.

They may have been stubborn, at first, insisting on their own way. But finally, they learned that it's in their own best interest to duplicate the pattern of success developed by the pioneers and fine-tuned by industry leaders over the years.

Look for someone who's a servant-leader. Look for someone who is passionate about their industry and what it can do for people in all walks of life. Look for someone who's making a difference. Look for someone who's courageous enough to share from their heart to lift others up from the muck and mire of empty survival-oriented, day-to-day living. Look for someone who may have been at the bottom, at least considerably less successful than they are now.

Look for someone who knows it's possible for anyone, who's hungry enough, to crawl out of the muddy waters of mediocrity. Look for someone who holds onto their leader or mentor until they gain the confidence to lead others into the blue skies and sunshine of success.

Look for someone who pinches themselves every day because they are, indeed, living the life they once only dreamed of. Look for someone who, every time you see or hear them sharing their story, is encouraging others.

Look for someone who reaches out and grabs your heart, enlivening your spirit with hope and the faith that *you can do it!* Look to them, listen to them; let them inspire you and help you motivate yourself. Then be like them and—*go do what they do!*

You too can be the champion that's deep in your heart; the one you've always known you could be. It's in the challenges that you find what you're made of. In the "valleys" is where you can grow the most so you can truly *SOAR* over the challenges. Dare yourself to *SOAR* and achieve your dreams!

Share your dreams and goals with your mentor or leader and possibly with other positive-thinking people who've given you unconditional support in the past. Ask them to support you as you compete against yourself.

You're growing into the industry leader you always knew you could be. You're beginning to surround yourself with other motivators who go for win-win situations every day— people who will help you stick to your goals.

As you grow and become, you develop into a fine leader yourself. Then, by your example, you give others who associate with you the hope they need to follow their dreams too.

8. Stop Making Excuses!

Always strive to exceed the initial goals you've set for yourself, even if it's just by a little bit. You don't always have to go an extra mile. Just strive to take an extra step or two, if that's all you can manage.

Here's the bottom line: always strive for at least a little something extra. It's a contagious attitude that is the mark of a person who wins! It rubs off on other people and other aspects of your life. It helps you develop a mind-set that helps you do your best to excel at everything that's important to you. It also attracts other budding leaders who'll follow your example and duplicate your success. It helps you to build a prosperous business or career, or whatever it is that you want.

9. Act on Fear!

Life isn't without its share of risks, and the higher you aim at reaching the stars, the more risks you're likely to encounter. Risk breeds fear—the bigger the risk, the more inclined you may be to avoid it. That's human nature. But, fear is the most debilitating emotion we possess. It's the biggest reason for there being so few people at the top!

And just remember this, fear can be thought of as two acronyms:

A. **F**alse **E**vidence **A**ppearing **R**eal—which means fear is simply a creation of the mind.

B. **F**orget **E**verything **A**nd **R**efocus—start fresh as if the fear doesn't exist.

Fear is simply something you hold in your mind. You might say it's a figment of your imagination. Let it go. To succeed, you need to take some chances, and overcome your fears. *You can't steal second base with one foot on first. Do things you fear, and fear will die.*

The bigger the chance you take and the less certain its outcome, the greater the feeling of accomplishment and satisfaction you get when you succeed. Even more, the further you extend out of your comfort (familiar) zone, the closer you will be to reaching the edge of your potential. As these "Act Now" guidelines reveal, there's nothing complicated about developing this mind-set. All that's required on your part is effort, and in that department everyone is truly created equal. *Attitude is the deciding factor in determining which efforts SOAR and which efforts sour.* The questions you need to ask yourself include the following:

> ➤ Do I have a winning, "Act Now" attitude?
> ➤ How much do I really want to succeed?
> ➤ Do I want it strongly enough to become a "Charlie Hustle" in my own endeavors, or is mediocre good enough for me?

Strike Now, or *Risk Striking Out!*

Developing an action-oriented attitude is simple, yet challenging. Life is full of distractions that can, if you allow them, sidetrack you from your mission. The secret is to avoid these situations from the outset—choose not to put yourself in situations where you have to make tough choices! As an example, parents often tell their children: "If you want a college education, get it right after high school graduation. If you put it off and start working for a living, you'll probably never go."

The same is true of becoming successful in your business or career. If you put off building your business or career, in favor of earning a little money at a part-time job, you are likely to get sidetracked. Life takes its twists and turns, and it can be a challenge to get back on track. You'd be favoring a little extra income now and probably spending it as fast as it comes in. You'd lose your edge and sacrifice a brighter future with the potential of financial freedom.

You'd find it too difficult to return to a lifestyle that doesn't include the weekly dinner out and the trinkets your part-time job enables you to buy. You'd fool yourself into thinking that you'll build your business or career some day, when you have the time. But, as we said earlier, some day turns into never and a lifetime of regrets about what could have been.

Strike while the iron's hot! This is an appropriate cliché borrowed from the annals of the blacksmith. It's much easier to mold metal into the shape you want immediately after removing it from the fire. Don't give it time to cool when it's more rigid and resistant to change. The sooner you build your business or career and, if your vehicle permits, get the time and money problem out of the way, the sooner you can live the life you've always yearned for.

Do it *now!* Go with what you've got when you've got it. There's no perfect time. But there's no time like the present. Act on it *now!* If you don't, you'll lose control over the shape of your future. You'll be reactive instead of proactive. Taking action just most of the time isn't going to get you to where you dream of being, either.

We creatures of habit tend to let most of the time slip into sometimes. Result: We don't achieve our goals. Don't set yourself up for regrets later on by failing to *act NOW! Commit yourself to your success!* Things are easier once you've eliminated the possibility of giving up or procrastinating. Procrastination is simply failure on the installment plan. It's what people do who don't live their dream.

Feed Your Mind *Act Now* Thoughts

If there's a common thread that binds all nine of the *ACT NOW* guidelines together, it's positive mental imaging—positive thinking in pictures. Your mind responds to what you feed it.

To condition yourself into becoming an action-oriented achiever, you need to constantly feed your mind positive *Act*

Now thoughts. See yourself succeeding—visualize it in your mind. Keep dreaming and, just as importantly, keep doing the things you know you need to do!

Your thinking, which includes your attitudes, are major determinants in whether or not you become an *Act Now* person. What does your attitude and thinking say about *you?* Are you ready to go? Are you fired up and ready for the success you're dreaming of?

Program your mind by repeating to yourself, over and over again, *"I'm a do-it-now person!"* Be aware of exactly how you use your time. Are you wisely *investing* your time, or just letting it go by?

Keep reminding yourself to manage your prioritized important activities. Be productive—not just busy!

Asking yourself questions like the ones below will make it easier to let go of any success-stealing habits you may have. Replace them with success-producing habits that keep you moving in the direction of your dreams.

"Act Now" Questions for Success

➤ Is this the best possible use of my time?
➤ Is this what I really need to be dong?
➤ Have I accomplished everything I set out to do today?

Patience and Flexibility—*Important Ingredients in the Action-Oriented Recipe*

It takes a high level of motivation and commitment to stick with your flight plan and strive for success. It also takes a high level of patience and flexibility. No matter how determined you might be in becoming an *Act Now* person, no one ever has complete control of one hundred percent of what can be done with their time.

Allow *flexibility* in your schedule. Things can and do happen along the way. Avoid scheduling yourself too tightly—allow a margin for error. But, at the same time, as soon as you've solved a challenge that came up, get yourself right back on track, following your plan. Using the distraction as an excuse will only delay your progress.

As Shakespeare once said, *"This, too, shall pass."* And, as Emerson said, *"Patience and fortitude conquer all things."*

The Achiever's Law

No matter how committed we are to making every hour of the day count, as we work toward our dreams, we still need to take care of the business of everyday living. The more we accept these things as a normal part of our lives, at least temporarily, the happier we are. Things such as making dinner, commuting to work, taking care of the children, cleaning up after a meal, routine home and property maintenance, paying bills—the duties of everyday life—can take up a great deal of time. Of course that doesn't even begin to take into consideration life's unforeseen calls to action such as: car repairs, health situations, pet messes, relationship challenges, and the like.

Yes, there are many aspects to life! And that's what helps make you strong along the way—balancing all your responsibilities while still *SOARING!*

So you may ask, "How can I *SOAR* to my dreams if I have so many distractions?" No one, even the wealthiest, is exempt from some distractions! It's your choice in how you respond to what needs to be done and what happens in your life. When you have a big enough dream, *nothing* can stop you from living it!

People who win in the game of life are good finders. They're possibility thinkers. They're solution oriented. They're forward moving. They keep their eyes on their goals and dreams as they handle their challenges. They create a positive approach like The Achiever's Law, which is: *"If anything good can happen it will, and at the best possible time!"* Do you believe this attitude is unrealistic? If so, just stop and consider this question for a moment. Did having a negative attitude about anyone or anything *ever* help you?

You may believe you're avoiding potential disappointment by being realistic. But remember, realistic is simply whatever you believe. Raise your belief level and develop the attitude that you can handle whatever happens in your life—that you can successfully deal with the worst-case scenario.

Why anticipate the worst? You'd just be setting yourself up for failure! Do people who *SOAR* to their dreams do that? I don't think so. People who win have positive expectations. That's how they attract positive thinking people into their lives. We *attract* what we think about.

Here is what some well-known people have said about positive thinking and self-fulfilling prophesies and actions:

> *"The thing always happens that you really believe in;*
> *And the belief in a thing makes it happen."*
> Frank Lloyd Wright

> *"The faultfinder will find faults even in paradise."*
> Henry David Thoreau

> *"Life is a mirror and will reflect back to the*
> *thinker what he thinks into it."*
> Ernest Holmes

> *"Change your thoughts and you change your world."*
> Norman Vincent Peale

Taking Charge

There are some things in life that we can't control. But we can always control our response to whatever happens. We can also control what everyday tasks or other jobs we can delegate to someone else. We can, for example, start by having a family meeting to discuss everyone's dreams. Then, we can decide what each person can do to contribute to the jobs that need to be done.

For example, let's say your child wants to participate in a certain after-school activity and you agree to it. He or she can then be responsible for finding transportation there and back, which may mean waiting for the after-school activity bus. A little inconvenience would help to make them stronger in the face of life's challenges, don't you agree? Besides, they could sit on the bench and do some homework while they wait!

Another key area of taking charge is to delegate unfruitful activities to others, so you can focus on your goal. For instance, you could have a neighborhood teenager, who's saving for college, cut your lawn and weed your garden each week for a reasonable price. He could perhaps wash your cars, and such, as well. What's your time worth? How much do you want your dreams and goals? If finances are a challenge, you need to accomplish more. Talk to your leader or mentor who knows your situation better and can advise you accordingly.

Maximize the Use of Your Time

Waiting in lines and doing routine chores and the like, can also be time you invest in yourself—your best investment! You can bring value to time spent waiting for appointments or service. And fortunately enough, it's simple and easy to do!

Whether you're doing something routine or taking care of an unexpected situation, you can invest otherwise unproductive time into a opportunity for continuing education. You can ask your leader or mentor to recommend books, videos, and audio tapes that'll help you reach the next level of achievement in your career or business. Always have a positive book with you in your briefcase, purse, or satchel. While you're waiting in line, pull the book out and read it.

You can also listen to audio tapes to help you get or stay motivated and build your skills. Make wise use of your commute time in the car or other times like in your bathroom getting ready for work or bed, or perhaps, when you're cooking a meal. Say you're on a stationary exercise bike, pedaling en route to better health. You can read a book, listen to a tape, or watch an inspiring video as you pedal! Even at the hairstylist's or barbershop, you can squeeze in some reading in many cases!

Take full advantage of these periods of otherwise empty time and control what you do with them! The people who win are *always* on the grow. They do their best to make each minute of each hour of each day count! It all adds up and helps to insure their success. How about you?

Success—*It's a Matter of Choice*

People who get things done—those people who *ACT*—are, more than anything else, people who *SEE* the best in life for themselves and their families. They *ORGANIZE* themselves with a plan to accomplish what they want and take the initiative to make sure that the best happens for them! They are passionate about living because of their strong desire to follow their dream—*whatever it takes*. Successful people *invest* their time in activities that will bring them closer to achieving their dreams. This often means they develop a mind-set that pushes them out the door when necessary.

When you have a mission to accomplish bigger and better things, then you too can be an *Act Now* person. Let go of any habits of procrastination, and your daily list of important accomplishments will grow. Watch yourself begin to take flight and *SOAR* above the crowd toward the destiny of your choosing.

Positive thinking is essential for success, but it isn't enough. Couple it with consistent positive action, though, and watch what happens! Nike's hook for their inspirational ad campaign said it best...

JUST DO IT!

Mental Exercise

What Grade Would You Give Yourself in the Following Subjects?

Grade

> I act immediately on important things that are a part of my plan...   _____
> I follow through with action on my goals...   _____
> I complete my goals on schedule...   _____
> I manage my activities effectively so I keep moving toward my goals...   _____
> I make positive use of empty time...   _____

"You will never stub your toe standing still. The faster you go (in the right direction), the more chance there is of stubbing your toe, but the more chance you have of getting where you want to go."

Charles F. Kettering

Chapter Summary

> Goals and plans are useful only when you take action!
> Keep pulling the *Act Now!* trigger. Let go of procrastination. Now is all you really have.
> Know when you are most productive. Take advantage of your "high tide." Avoid Dormancy Dungeons—know your escapes and *ACT!*
> Divide and conquer—break up big projects into smaller ones, then begin!
> On a daily basis, write down and prioritize items that you need to do. Refer to the list regularly, as you focus on do-

ing the important things first and delegating what you can.

➤ Let go of making excuses, even if you have an unexpected situation to resolve. Keep following your plan. Get right back on track.

➤ Share your goals with your leader or mentor and supportive family members or friends, so they can help you remain accountable.

➤ Always strive to do something extra beyond your goal!

➤ *ACT*, even if you're afraid.

➤ Feed your mind *Act Now!* thoughts.

➤ Invest in yourself with continuing education, by reading positive books and listening to positive tapes, during otherwise unproductive empty time.

A Final Reflection on *ACTING*...

"To dream anything that you want to dream. That is the beauty of the human mind. To do anything that you want to do. That is the strength of the human will. To trust yourself to test your limits. That is the courage to succeed."

Bernard Edmonds

Chapter 7

REJECTING YOUR WAY TO SUCCESS.
FAILURE IS NOT AN OPTION—
REJECT IT

*"If you have made mistakes, even serious
ones, there is always another chance for you.
What we call failure is not the falling
down, but the staying down."*
Mary Pickford

Turning Setbacks Upside Down

Finally, we've come down to *R*—the fourth and ever-so-important last letter in *SOAR*.

"Wait a minute!" you might be saying, "We know we need to *SEE* the dream, *ORGANIZE* it into a plan of attack, and then *ACT* on it...sounds like all the elements are there." All except one.

Failure is a fact of life. We all fail periodically. In fact, the more successful you are, the more likely you've failed a lot in the process! Setbacks do come. Sweet dreams can turn sour but only if you *allow* those first obstacles and early defeats to turn your optimistic hopes and high expectations into puffs of smoke. Some give up their pursuit of going for the "gold" when they begin realizing the long odds against them.

Even the greatest dreams, plans, and actions eventually lead to nothing—if we allow failure to turn us back along the way. Remember, it isn't what happens to you in life that determines whether or not you achieve your dreams. Instead, what matters most is how you *respond* to what happens to you. That's what really determines your future.

R stands for *REJECTING*. Rejecting failure. Rejecting misfortune. Rejecting negative circumstances. Rejecting dream deflating comments and behavior.

Very few words are so seriously perceived and, as a result, have as harsh an impact as the word *REJECTING*. When it comes to overcoming failure, *you need to absolutely refuse to settle for unwanted results.* Sure, the word *REJECTING* is harsh, but so is failure. For those who want to succeed, *failure is not an option.* They just keep going until they accomplish their goal.

To be successful, you need to turn failures into opportunities to learn and become stronger in the process. You need to look at failures as steps along the way that take you closer to making your dreams come true. Don't give up! Keep on keeping on. Reject temporary stumbling blocks. Reject the noes. Reject defeats! These things are just tests of your commitment! Once you pass enough of these tests, you get your reward—your dream becomes reality!

Sir Edmund Hillary did...

After numerous failed attempts at climbing the world's tallest mountain, some of which claimed the lives of fellow explorers, Edmund Hillary proclaimed, *"Everest, you have beaten us, but we will conquer. You cannot grow bigger, but we can."*

To winners, failing is not used as an excuse for quitting, but rather as a lesson for learning, and thus, better equipping themselves to overcome the next obstacle. Experience, it's been said, is what you get when you didn't get what you wanted! And experience teaches us that *"winners never quit, and quitters never win."* As B.C. Forbes once said...

"Call the roll in your memory of conspicuously
successful business giants and...you will be struck
by the fact that almost every one of them encountered
inordinate difficulties sufficient to crush all but the
gamest of spirits. Edison went hungry many
times before he became famous."

Mental Exercise

When was the last time you stopped pursuing something you really wanted?

➤ What stopped you?
➤ Was it failure after the first attempt?
➤ What exactly was it that caused you to "pull in the reins?"

What happens if obstacles arise that threaten to impair your vision of success? What do you do if circumstances prevent you from following the carefully thought-out plans you've developed for yourself? How do you keep on going when your mountains seem unconquerable? Is your first inclination to quit or is it to *REJECT* failure?

No matter how hard you work, unlimited success is never guaranteed. You can improve your odds, but you cannot control them altogether. Why? No matter how thoroughly you develop your goals and plans, and no matter how carefully you look at all the angles, unforeseen challenges will arise.

Since you are the pilot in command of your own aircraft, you are responsible for guiding it to your dream. As you *SOAR,* you will undoubtedly encounter turbulence, shifts in wind direction, rain, low visibility, ice, down drafts, and other variables that test your navigating abilities. No matter what you may encounter, though, you will do whatever it takes to follow your flight plan and stay on course.

Similarly, all of our lives are subject to a multitude of variables over which we have no direct control. Every second of every day, there are thousands of events taking place. And even though we can't predict them, they can affect our lives in some way whether we realize it or not.

Consider the hustle and bustle of a typical business day in the heart of New York City. Picture all those people walking with, around, and sometimes even over each other in a frenzied "ant-hill" of activity on the streets. Some of them are chasing their dreams, just like you. At a minimum, they are probably intent on reaching a destination to meet someone or do something.

With all these people going in millions of different directions, is it any wonder the landscape of humanity is in a constant state of change? And New York is just *one* city! What about London, England? Or Sydney, Australia? The larger the population gets, the more variables there are to deal with, and the more things change.

Rapid change has become a constant. There are many things happening that you have no control over. Therefore, everything won't always fall into place exactly as planned. You've already noticed that, haven't you? And as you may know, there's even an expression that fairly well sums up the situation...

"Stuff" Happens!

It's unavoidable. In all of our lives, at one time or another, "stuff" happens. It is precisely at this point that the winners and the whiners come to the proverbial fork in the road and part company.

In line with their unswerving persistence, winners are notably flexible. They adjust to setbacks, and they look for another route toward their dream. Maybe they just need to take a temporary detour.

Winners also reject the negative mind-set that "wanna-bes" so frequently accept. They look for other positive-thinking people to associate with. They understand that *teamwork makes the dream work.* They understand that success is never guaranteed, but their odds are magnified many times over when they persevere.

As Longfellow once said, *"The heights by great men reached and kept were not attained by sudden flight, but they, while their companions slept, were toiling upward in the night."*

Tackling Obstacles with Wood-Splitting Determination— *There's No Such Thing as Try!*

How many times have you had somebody attempt to console you over a setback or failure in your life by saying this: "Well, at least you gave it your best shot. You *tried*, and that's all that matters." What these people fail to realize is that success is a cumulative process—as you take action toward your goal, events build on top of one another until you reach it. *Trying* doesn't "cut" it!

It's similar to when we're splitting a piece of wood in two with an axe. Those of us who don't have Paul Bunyan, the legendary giant lumberjack, in our family lineage probably have to swing the axe more than once to split a log in half. Say you swing the axe twice, and both times you put everything you can muster into the swing. Still, the piece of wood hasn't split. You've given it your two best shots, but you haven't finished the job.

Would you quit now, satisfied in knowing you *tried* your best? Of course not! Why? Because you know that you'll probably be picking up toothpicks in another swing or two. As Einstein once said, *"People love chopping wood: in this task, one sees immediate results."* Once again, *trying* doesn't cut it!

Using another example, persistence has helped us to loosen the lid on a jar. The lid refused to come off on the first attempt. And the second. And the third. Now you know that you just need one more good, strong twist to get it open—so you keep at it. It may take three more efforts, but you stick with it anyway.

Success is the same way! *Reject failures that keep you from taking the lid off your dreams!* Don't just go through the motions and give up after a few good tries. Keep going! You never know—you might be just one twist away from success! *Remember, there's no such thing as try. You either do something or you don't!*

Self-Confidence—*A Powerful Force*

George Lucas elegantly displayed this winning philosophy in *Return of the Jedi*, one of the films in his classic *Star Wars* science fiction trilogy. Before being endowed with the wisdom of the Jedi, young Luke Skywalker was frustrated at his repeated failures to master his control of The Force. Yoda, the frail, unassuming Master who took it upon himself to put Luke through Jedi University, preached of practice and the virtues of a positive mental attitude. But Luke, consumed by a burning passion to quickly rise to the rank of Jedi Master, would complain about his apparent lack of progress and question Yoda's teaching methods.

Although Luke had big dreams *(SEEING)*, sought out a mentor *(ORGANIZING)*, and passionately set about pursuing *(ACTING)* these dreams, he became easily discouraged when success wasn't achieved on his first few attempts. His frustrations led him to question the value of Yoda's teachings. Yoda ultimately demonstrates the true "Force" of his methods by elevating Luke's spaceship with his little finger and some intense concentration—no strings, no wires, no kidding...

> Luke: "I don't believe it!"
> Yoda: "*That* is why you fail."
> (Yoda uses this event as leverage in convincing Luke to REJECT failure.)
> Luke: "Okay, I'll try..."
> Yoda: "No! Do not try! Do, or do not. There *is* no try."

If at First You Don't Succeed...

Yoda's message is a strong one—putting forth a lot of effort is admirable, but why put forth any effort if you're ultimately going to quit and not achieve your objective anyway? *Succeeding the first time out isn't that important. But succeeding is! If at first you don't succeed, keep going...* Again, and again if necessary. Failure is not an option!

Keep doing—until you succeed—then keep doing some more. Perseverance and the ability to *REJECT* failure are traits that are absolutely crucial in the makeup of top achievers.

You are lucky, because in the next 30 seconds you can benefit from the knowledge it took Yoda over 600 years to accumulate. Repeat after me...

I Keep Going.
"I Keep Going!"
I Have No Excuses.
"I Have No Excuses!"

Decide right now to commit to Yoda's philosophy. Do whatever is necessary to reach your goal—*no excuses!* Commit yourself to achieving the results you want by *REJECTING* failed attempts and setbacks as excuses to quit. You'll be amazed at how determined you can become once you remove the possibility of quitting as an option.

Instead of negatively thinking, "Well, I guess it just wasn't meant to be," and then forgetting about your goal when you incur a setback, *change your perspective!* Assume a successful positive-thinking frame of mind by telling yourself, "Okay, it wasn't meant to be *this* time, but I've learned from the experience, and I'll do better *next* time. *I'm going to persist until I make it happen."*

Luke ultimately became a Jedi Master. It wasn't easy, and it didn't happen overnight, but take a look at him now! The Force is with him. The Force we earthlings call Success can be with you, too, when you truly believe it can be and settle for nothing less!

Seeing the Positive Light

To *SOAR* to new heights that initially seem very lofty and distant, count on having challenges along the way. Enjoying the journey while overcoming them, one by one, leads you to your treasured goal or dream.

People who succeed grow from their failed attempts. In essence, they look at failure as a learning event rather than a reflection of themselves or someone else. Thomas Edison, one of the greatest inventors in history, was once asked why he continued to bother toiling over an invention that he repeatedly failed to make work. His reply, *"Because I have now discovered one thousand ways it won't work."* To succeed, we need to look at our setbacks in the same positive light.

Look at baseball. Even the best hitters are successful only three out of every 10 times they step up to the plate. Baseball players know there is a fine line between success and failure, and that every success (a hit) will inevitably be followed by failures (outs). Most people can recall that Mark McGwire made the record books by hitting 70 homeruns during the 1998 season. But nobody remembers all the times he struck out. And neither does he!

Granted, failure is not fun. I'm not implying that you should just walk away from a failed effort saying, "Well, it's okay that I failed, because I learned something." Winners are people who, in every aspect of their lives, want to exceed their own personal best because they're passionate about succeeding. They want to finish first—it's the most exciting challenge. Yet they know that their only real race is with themselves. They don't like to fail on themselves!

Never settle for anything less than everything you want. But if you fail—and when you consistently set your goals high enough, you probably will fail sometimes—view those failures with a positive frame of mind. That's what *REJECTING* failure is all about!

Wear Self-Confidence Like a "Walkman" Portable Radio!

Early on when you're working to overcome the initial obstacles and succeed, keeping yourself in a positive frame of mind is simple—but not always easy. Keeping a positive out-look in a world filled with negative-thinking people is one of the greatest challenges that anyone with the will to win must endure.

Above all else, you need to believe in yourself! *Become passionate about succeeding by believing in your dreams and committing yourself to their eventual success, regardless of what "experts" and well-meaning friends might say.* Believe in your-self. Listen to yourself. Wear self-confidence like a Walkman—plug into a can do attitude and drown out the nega-tive voices. Remember, the log will split in two when you just keep swinging. You will win when you just keep doing. Former U.S. President Abraham Lincoln did.

The World's Greatest Role Model of Persistence
Abraham Lincoln, the sixteenth President of the United States, is one of the world's greatest examples of what it means to get knocked down and then get right back up again. Consider Lincoln's rocky road of success. Ask yourself how you can develop persistence so you, too, have the confidence to keep on go-ing...no matter what! As Lincoln once said, *"I do the very best I know how—the very best I can; and I mean to keep on doing so until the end."*

A Portrait of Success

Failed in Business—Bankruptcy, 1831
Defeated for Legislature, 1832
Failed in Business, 1835
Sweetheart/Fiancé Dies, 1835
Nervous Breakdown, 1836
Defeated in Election, 1838
Defeated for U.S. Congress, 1843
Defeated Again for U.S. Congress, 1846

Defeated Once Again for U.S. Congress, 1848
Defeated for U.S. Senate, 1855
Defeated for U.S. Vice President, 1856
Defeated Again for U.S. Senate, 1858
Elected President of the U.S., 1860

"Always bear in mind that your own resolution to succeed
is more important than any other one thing."

And...

"You cannot fail...unless you quit!"
Abraham Lincoln

Mental Exercise

Not many people, at their current level of development,
would have the strength and fortitude to carry on if faced
with a similar set of circumstances as Lincoln was. How
about you? What would you do if you were faced with a
series of similar hardships? How would you bolster
your attitude of persistence to keep on going?

Lincoln's story is encouraging. As you strive for what you want and run into obstacles, shrug off the notion that it just isn't meant to be, that some goals aren't meant to be attained. Ask yourself whether you've really given the attainment of your goal a fair chance. Are you giving up before you've explored all the solutions to your challenges en route to your dream?

Talent, brains, athletic prowess, and such are marvelous things to be blessed with, but you can't always rely on them. *Talent comes and goes with different success stories, but persistence is a constant. Persistence is what delivers!*

Persistence Pays Off in a Big Way!

As Helen Keller once said, *"We can do anything we want to when we stick to it enough."* Such persistence paid off for "Honest Abe" in a big way. It usually does. Colonel Sanders, of Kentucky Fried Chicken fame, is now a household name, at least in the U.S. But there was a time when, believe it or not, *nobody* would endorse his chicken recipe! He got rejected 1,009 times, but he persisted. Movie Director Steven Spielberg, business giant Lee Iacocca, computer wizard Bill Gates, and inventor Thomas Edison—they all persisted. And the list goes on.

Stories about talented people who never made it past being "Mr. Potential" are all too common. But you rarely hear stories about persistent people failing. Where do you stand? Would your friends describe you as "Mr. Potential" or "Mr. Persistence"?

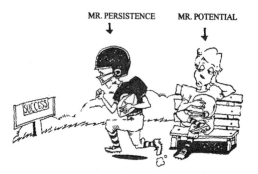

The Only Expert About You is *You!*

"When you're truly committed to success, nobody can stop you," remarked U.S. actor and comedian Robin Williams in describing his own ascent to stardom. To witness Robin's incredible gift for improvisation, you'd never guess he was rather withdrawn and straight-laced throughout much of his youth—and voted by his high school class as the least likely to succeed! But somewhere around his senior year in high school, he heard his calling. More importantly, he heeded it. How do you suppose Robin Williams'

high school counselor responded when Robin said, "I'm going to be a stand-up comic"? Chances are, Robin overcame the advice of this expert and a few others. He followed *his* dream.

We all need to "stop selling ourselves short." Most of us underestimate our abilities. Paula Abdul didn't sell herself short when one choreographer after another kept telling her she was too short (5"2") to be a dancer. But her work ethic put her on top of the entertainment world. Although she's one of the most multi-talented people in the industry, talent *alone* didn't get her to the top. *REJECTING* failure did. Luckily, for all the people who enjoy her work so much, she decided to reject the opinions of the "experts" and stretch herself to make her dream happen.

There will undoubtedly be people who don't think you can do something. Such nay-sayers are all too prevalent! But what do *you* believe? That's what is really important. Maybe you're not sure if you can do it or not. That's okay, but just remember, *it's only when you stretch yourself that you begin to discover that the limit of your true potential is farther out there than you might have imagined.* I think of this as "The Rubber Band Axiom." It goes like this...

Rubber Band Axiom

A rubber band, left lying around on a counter top somewhere, doesn't do anything. But once picked up and stretched, it becomes useful. Once stretched and let go, it gains the potential to fly over much greater distances than before.

Are *you* stretching yourself? Christopher Columbus certainly did. Columbus, looking to find a shorter route to the East Indies by going west, endured nonstop hardships during his voyage that led to near mutiny on a daily basis. Despite repeated setbacks, and in the face of conventional "wisdom" (i.e., The Earth is flat, Chris. Your obsession with a round world will drive you over the edge!), Columbus set his course in the direction that his own inspiration and intelligence led him to believe was the right one.

If the "FUD" (Fear, Uncertainty, and Doubt) Factor casts a shadow in your direction, find your own inspiration in the words Columbus entered into his private log. During his quest across the uncharted North Atlantic, he wrote...

"This day, we sailed on."

Mental Exercise

As Columbus Knew All Too Well, a Ship in the Harbor Is Usually Safe—But That's Not What Ships Were Built for. What Were YOU *Built for? What Great Accomplishments Still Remain Undone Because You Have Not Rejected Failure?*

Invest the time NOW to renew your commitment to overcoming past failures, including fears that have prevented you from taking action in the first place! Go ahead and give yourself a chance to succeed by taking another shot—or two, or three. Who knows? One more effort could be all you need to get on the right course.

Chapter Summary

Chart a Bold Course for Yourself...And Sail On!
➤ It's how you deal with failures that counts; not the failures themselves.
➤ Succeeding the first time you do something isn't important—doing it until you succeed is.
➤ Nothing can take the place of persistence in achieving your goals.
➤ Learn from your failed attempts.

➤ Every log will eventually split when you keep on swinging the axe.
➤ Wear self-confidence like a "Walkman" portable radio.
➤ Abide by "The Rubber Band Axiom" and *s-t-r-e-t-c-h* yourself!
➤ Don't let the "FUD" (Fear, Uncertainty, Doubt) Factor shadow your efforts.
➤ Sail on...

A Final Reflection on *REJECTING*...

"Nothing in this world can take the place of persistence. Talent will not; nothing is more common than unsuccessful men with talent. Genius will not; unrewarded genius is almost a proverb. Education will not; the world is full of educated derelicts. Persistence and determination alone are omnipotent. The slogan 'press on' has solved and always will solve the problems of the human race."
Calvin Coolidge

"Circumstances don't make the person, they reveal who he is."
Horace

Chapter 8

YOU'RE THE PILOT OF YOUR OWN SUCCESS

"Our daily objective needs to be to grow and become each day as we SOAR toward our dreams."
Shawn Anderson

You Now Possess the Secret

Achieving your goals and dreams in life is knowing how to *SOAR,* and doing it!

> ➤ *Success begins when you SEE your dream and what you want to accomplish in as much detail as possible.*

> ➤ *Success is bolstered when you ORGANIZE attaining your dream into a specific, workable plan.*

> ➤ *Success becomes possible when you ACT on that plan with resolute determination.*

> ➤ *Success become probably when you REJECT failure and all momentary setbacks that could impede the ultimate achievement of your dream.*

With these four principles, you now know the basic secrets of the great achievers. Anyone who lives their dream has the four principles of *SOAR* deeply imbedded in the core of their thinking and behavior—whether they know it or not!

But you have one advantage they may not! You have a success formula you can continually plug yourself into time and time again—whatever your goal might be. You can examine how you're advancing toward any goal by objectively analyzing your progress, by using the principles of *SOAR—SEEING, ORGANIZING, ACTING,* and *REJECTING.*

> ➤ If your purpose is cloudy or you're uncertain about your objective, focus on *SEEING*.

> ➤ If the steps seem unclear as to what you need to be doing to fulfill your dreams, concentrate on *ORGANIZING*.

> ➤ If you're making progress toward the accomplishment of your goal, set your attention to *ACTING*.

> ➤ If you're working your plan diligently and passionately but success fails to greet your effort, persist by *REJECTING* failure.

So, there it is. You now know the secret of how to *SOAR* in life:

SEEING—ORGANIZING—ACTING—REJECTING

Simple, yet powerful. Easy, yet life-changing.

Now that you know the secret, it's your time to choose.

1. *Do you want the best life has to offer?*
2. *Are you willing to commit one hundred percent—mentally, emotionally, and physically—in order to accomplish your dreams?*

Making your dreams a reality requires passion—a deep-down, in-your-heart, *burning desire*. It's this sort of desire that demands a monthly, weekly, and daily commitment to being your best and doing your best. This requires consistently growing through a continuing education program and taking the required action. Happiness is a choice, and fulfillment isn't something that automatically happens—you have to want them—and work for them! How? They are byproducts of following your dream.

Life is an active journey, and a rich life experience is the result of consistent, focused effort. When you want great things to happen for you, you have to strive for great things.

Giving lip service and telling others you want the best just isn't enough. Telling yourself you want and desire the best—whatever that is for you—is a start. Then going after your dreams wholeheartedly, until you get them, is what it takes.

So, what is *your* choice? Are you going to "walk the walk" or just "talk the talk?" Only you can decide.

The truth is, *life is too precious and too short not to do what you're passionate about.* Sure, we might not achieve all of our dreams, but the magic of life is in always having bigger dreams to chase.

Whether your goal is to build a business, raise first-rate children, empower a million people to live with more passion, or something else, life becomes more thrilling when you pursue your dreams. Life takes on a different level of vitality when you're motivated. You're excited, your eyes sparkle, and you move confidently.

Dreams Should Never Become Wishes

Some people might argue that they don't have enough time, or that it is too late for them to *SOAR* in life. The only way to respond to this is to asks yourself, "If in the last days of my life I were to reflect upon everything I did and didn't do, will I have more regrets at having *SOARED*, or not?

The answer seems rather clear when the question is asked with the end of the line in mind, doesn't it? As long as you're still alive, you can *SOAR!*

Achiever Profile: Victory Is Often Only "One" Race Away

A young jockey lost his first race, his second, his third, his first ten, his first twenty. But he kept striving. He lost his first 100 races, his first 200. But he kept plugging away—and lost 50 more. After 250 straight losses, Eddie Arcaro won his first race. He went on to become the most famous jockey of his era.

The Smart Money Says...

Chip away as quickly as you can, but even if you need to slow down for a time...still keep chipping away as much as you can!

"I will do today as others will not, so I can live tomorrow as others cannot."
Author Unknown

REJECT all excuses and put *ACTION* into your dreams! Start working toward your goal with whatever time you can devote to it—then increase that time increment as you go. The *key* is to *start* working on it! Whether you move ahead rapidly or an inch at a time, you'll reach the finish line when you keep working for what you want.

Even small, steady, persistent steps taken toward the achievement of your goal will pay off. As professional speaker and author Ty Boyd says, *"Success is determined by taking the hand you were dealt and utilizing it to the very best of your ability."*

Put the "Multiplier Effect" to Work for You
Take a look at the example below:

$$3 \times 3 \times 3 \times 3 \times 3 = 243$$
$$4 \times 4 \times 4 \times 4 \times 4 = 1{,}024$$

Certainly, it's a small step from three to four. But over time, the difference between the two numbers grows dramatically! The same multiplying power demonstrated here can also be applied to everyday living!

Imagine the possibilities if you were to go the extra mile to increase your effectiveness each day by 33 percent from a three to a four! Picture the great things you could achieve when you take advantage of the power of the "Multiplier Effect" in your own life. Spending twenty more minutes writing, making five extra sales calls, or doing 50 more sit-ups. This sort of extra-mile activity will begin to create the momentum that will accelerate you toward the realization of your dream.

By maximizing your performance every day, you create a situation where positive things start happening. You get closer to finishing writing a book, you make one more big sale this month over last, you bring on another business associate, or you lose another pound.

The power of the Multiplier Effect is put into full force by your doing just *a little more every day* toward the achievement of your dream. Those that truly *SOAR* do! There is nothing magical about it. It's the power of persistence—by *ACTING* on your dreams with invincible determination...daily, weekly, monthly, yearly...*you will produce results.* That steady series of small successes each day will begin to build, multiply, and grow into something much bigger! As Emerson once said, *"Guard well your spare moments. They are like uncut diamonds. Discard them and their value will never be known. Improve them and they will become the brightest gems in a useful life."*

How to Guarantee That the *Multiplier Effect* Will Change Your Life

Unfortunately, it's not uncommon for people to let goals and dreams fall by the wayside. How about you? Have you ever done that?

The key difference with the great majority of people is how they respond when they run into the brick wall of everyday life. You notice that I *didn't* say *if* they run into the "brick wall." We all run into it sooner or later!

It is undeniable that the achievement of your goals requires an investment of your time, commitment, and energy. Everyday living, if we allow it to, can sap us of all three of these elements.

Money concerns, car challenges, unappreciative employers, what to make for dinner are just some of the many different situations and events that keep us busy, and potentially side-tracked if we permit it. People, by and large, need to give more to maintaining their focus or purpose.

Sure, reading a motivational book, listening to a tape, or attending a seminar can help you regain your balance and stay on track. As you may have noticed though, *Rocky* theme music, for instance, as well as other music that helps you get fired up, can carry you only so far.

Short-term motivational "hits" from others, although they play a part in the recipe of success, do not produce long-term results. We need more ingredients.

So, what do you need to do to produce long-term results? What do you do to encourage yourself to be consistently committed to peak performance? You need to understand one of the great "Laws of Success." Simply stated, it says:

"Personal success is a personal responsibility."

To put the Multiplier Effect to work and help you maintain the passion necessary to push you through to the most distant finish lines, you need to hold yourself accountable. One of the greatest steps you can take to help you achieve the passions of your heart is to keep an accountability journal or, as I refer to it, a performance journal.

Your Performance Journal—*The Monitoring Tool That Encourages Results*

Keeping a performance journal takes effort and commitment. But isn't maintaining an unsatisfactory status quo energy-consuming as well? It is a tool, however, that can help you get and stay "off the ground," setting you free to perform, to achieve, to enjoy, and to win. It provides you with a place to record your goals, your plans, your actions, and your successes and failures. In fact, if you already have a day planner or organizer, you're all set—you can use that as your performance journal. Having and using a performance journal allows you to *SOAR* to new heights!

Monitoring your performance and the results you get is what successful businesses do every day. Consistent and measured tracking of accounting, marketing, and sales are just three areas that keep winning businesses humming along at peak levels. *By tracking performance regularly, decision-makers are able to determine if their business is heading in the right direction.* They know to what degree the business is making progress toward monthly, quarterly, and yearly goals.

Tracking your individual successes can be done the same way. By monitoring the results of your daily actions, you, too, can detect if you're making progress in the pursuit of your dreams. You will be able to tell if you are moving forward or backward in the pursuit of your goals. You are either moving forward in life or backward in life. It's as simple as that—there is no middle ground. Even those who believe they are maintaining are losing precious time. The time on their life clock shows no mercy as it continues to tick.

By consistently inventing time to evaluate your progress and then taking action based on what you learn, you are going to notice positive change. It may be subtle at first, but you are going to notice improvement taking place in your life. As you continue this habit, you'll notice dramatic improvement.

At YOU, Inc., *You're in Charge!*

Think of yourself as the Chairman of the Board of one of the most powerful companies every created—YOU, Inc. You also happen to be the CEO (Chief Executive Officer), the CFO (Chief Financial Officer), the Vice President of Marketing, and the Director of Human Resources. You are everything! You are 100 percent responsible for the performance of YOU, Inc.

Of course, being in control means taking responsibility for your performance. That means you need to monitor your progress. Businesses that don't track performance limit their success. And, people who don't monitor their progress limit *their* success. That can be quite motivating, so here it is again!

People who don't monitor their progress limit their success.

As former President and founding father of the U.S., Thomas Jefferson said, *"Eternal vigilance is the price of liberty."*

Goal Resolutions—*Once a Year or Once a Day?*

Most people focus on their goals once a year. Using a performance journal, you will have the opportunity to do it every day. A performance journal helps you create habits. Good habits. Successful habits.

Things get better in life by change, not chance. For things to change in your life, you need to realize that *you* must change. Personal mastery is found in taking action. *And one of the most powerful actions you can take is monitoring your own attitude and behavior in line with your dreams and goals.*

Mental Exercise

Let me ask you a life-changing question...

"Are your goals important enough that you are willing to commit to them every day?"

You need to know that both answers, Yes or No, have definite consequences:

If You Answered *Yes*

You've increased your potential further than you can currently imagine.

If You Answered *No*

You'd better be extremely lucky or incredibly talented because you've just communicated to yourself that you're not willing to give 100 percent in the pursuit of your goal.

Of course, it would be great if every one of you answered Yes! But that's highly unlikely. For a variety of reasons, some people decide to limit their ability to *SOAR*, and thus, limit their opportunity to maximize their potential. I hope you're not one of them. To win in the game of life, just say YES!

Do You Want to Rise Above the Crowd? *Then Take the Next Step*

For those willing to give it their all—to do whatever it takes, I have included *The SOAR Performance Journal*. It highlights a terrific self-accountability tool that will help you put into action every element of *SOAR*.

The SOAR Performance Journal can be the catalyst that will push you over the top. It will help you achieve your goals  and directs you to a life of adventure and deep satisfaction. It is a unique tool that will help you solidify your dreams and drive you to action. It is your own personal flight plan that will guide you to a life of purpose and passion.

Living an empowered life does require effort. Achieving your dreams does require commitment. Do you agree that your life is too important to settle for anything less? I believe that about you—how about *you?* Even if you just *want* to believe it, that's a great start.

Blaze Your Own Trails Through Life and Go for It Now! *If Not Now—Then When?* There Is No Perfect Time

You can, you know. By integrating the four principles of *SOAR* into your mind and heart, you can start blazing exciting and life-changing trails, even if you've never done so before. Similar to great adventurers of the past and present, you, too, can embark on a life of adventure, excitement, and challenge—whatever that is for you. Now that you've armed yourself with a powerful machete called *SOAR*, you can start clearing trails with unmistakable clarity.

Cut through the failures of your past and toss them aside while remembering what you've learned. Head with confidence in the direction you want to go. Head toward your goals and dreams. Just remember to keep hacking away—at even the thickest brush. You'll clear the path, and obstacles will eventually fall by the wayside!

Each Day Is a Gift—*Make Each One Count*

In this busy world of ours, we often forget to appreciate the excitement each day holds. Each new rising of the sun offers so much opportunity! *SOAR* helps us remember that great careers and businesses are built *one step at a time*, and great lives *one day at a time*.

By intentionally living every day to the fullest, great things can happen—to you, your co-workers, your associates, your neighbors, and to anybody else who becomes resolute in their determination to *SOAR*.

I wish you all the best along your journey in life. I hope that, in some small way, I have inspired you to give serious thought to your potential—to acknowledge the value of your life. I hope I have sparked your desire to lead a more passionate and purposeful life.

Without even knowing you, I can honestly say that I believe in you. I believe in your ability to accomplish great things. How so? Because I believe in the power of the human spirit—a spirit capable of *SOARING* to extraordinary heights.

Your life is a fairy tale that continues to be written every day. Reach for your potential! Seize your own destiny and make your life a brilliant *SOARING* success.

SOARING

*When you're
SOARING, you're
giving the best you
can give. You're loving
yourself and your family
enough to make your goals
and dreams come true. And you
know you deserve your dreams.
When you're SOARING, you're loving
others whom you meet on your flight, as
you're giving to the world through what
you're doing. You're leading the way for
others by your shining example—
giving them hope that they, too,
can SOAR. And last but not
least, because of your
loving contribution to
the world, you are
making a positive
difference in the
lives of others.*

Chapter 9

HOW TO USE
THE SOAR PERFORMANCE JOURNAL

*"Nothing will come of nothing.
Dare mighty things."*
Shakespeare

The Four Parts

This accountability log is made up of four essential parts. And for easy access, it can be made a part of your day planner or organizer. It's a way to expand upon what you may already be doing. Use tabs to separate these four sections and put fresh sheets of paper in each section every week.

Recommended Time Investment

➤ *For best results, fill out The SOAR Performance Journal nightly*—which takes only five to ten minutes. This includes completing the *SEEING* and *ORGANIZING* sections on Sunday evening and the *ACTING* and *RE-JECTING* sections every night. Additionally, you also need to invest about 10 to 20 minutes at the end of each week. You could also do this on Sunday evening, reviewing the results of that week. This brief investment of time can help you reap tremendous rewards.

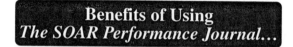

Benefits of Using
The SOAR Performance Journal...

➤ *It encourages you to have daily accountability.* When you complete it in the evening and glance at it in the morning, *The SOAR Performance Journal* helps you keep your goals firmly etched in your mind. By focusing on your goals every day, they come alive for you and you become more deeply committed to their accomplishment.

➤ *It helps you develop the mind-set of an achiever.* The *SOAR Performance Journal* is not a diary. It's simply a factual documentation of the successes and failures of your day as they affect the achievement of your goal. It helps you stay focused on taking the necessary daily actions that will progressively lead to the realization of your dream. It assists you in changing your goals into something you're actually working for rather than something you're merely wishing would happen "someday."

➤ *It is a learning tool.* By studying the details of your successes and failures, you develop insight into your personal strengths and weaknesses. Through acquiring a deeper understanding of your own thinking and actions, you give yourself the opportunity to grow and learn...and make the necessary attitude or other changes that will enable you to be successful.

How to Effectively Use
The SOAR Performance Journal

➤ *For each current goal you have, keep a separate sheet.* Set your sights on working on no more than two or three major goals at a time. By working on too many goals at once, you limit the attention you can give to a specific goal, therefore limiting your success.

➤ *Analyze your results weekly.* At the end of each week, invest the time necessary to review your journal. Study your progress. Study your successes and failures. Notice the consistencies and inconsistencies. Use the information to help you avoid making the same mistakes over again.

➤ *Analyze trends monthly.* Look back over the previous month's recordings and look for trends...when you're on track and what caused you to be off track. Be objective and honest with yourself. Use a different color pen to circle and highlight anything that stands out in your mind. With *The SOAR Performance Journal,* you're tracking your life, so invest the time to review the information you record. Analyze your strengths and weaknesses, learn from them, and fine-tune your skills as you go along.

1 The *SEEING* Section

➤ *The SEEING Section reminds you to put your goals down on paper...every week.* This is a very powerful exercise that can help you build strong momentum toward your goals. It can also help you think about the pleasure that will come with accomplishing your goal—or the pain you're likely to experience by not accomplishing your goal. This association of both pleasure and pain to your goal can be very motivating.

➤ *The SEEING Section encourages you to associate positive and negative emotions with your goals.* People usually have a tendency to go toward pleasure and away from pain. That's one reason why you always need to keep your goals in front of you—so you can focus on the positive results you're working toward. As you start a new sheet of paper each week, invest some time thinking about the words you write in the *SEEING* section. Although your goal is likely to remain the same for awhile, do not go on "autopilot." Don't just copy the list of feelings and thoughts associated with your goal from the previous week without feeling them again. The more you get in touch with your heartfelt feelings and focus on the pleasure and pain aspects of your goal, the more intense the desire for your goal will become. Your passion will increase and this will help you *SOAR* over, through, and around your obstacles!

Here are some areas to consider when selecting goals to pursue:

➤ **Continuing Education**—*What do you need or want to learn? What books, tapes, seminars, training, and such are available to you?*

➤ **Career**—*What career path do you find motivating? Do you want to move on?*

➤ **Job**—*How is your performance in your current job?*

➤ **Business**—*Is building a business the key to living your dreams?*

➤ **Money**—*Do you need to increase your income to buy that new car, home, or something else?*

➤ **Exercise**—*Are you tired of feeling worn out?*

➤ **Weight**—*Does being ten pounds lighter sound appealing?*

➤ **Spiritual**—*Do you want to develop a deeper relationship with God?*

➤ **Relationships**—*How about improving the quality of your family and other relationships?*

➤ **Family**—*Would you like to be a full-time parent?*

➤ **Attitudes**—*What can you do to eliminate any negative attitudes and be more positive?*

➤ **Habits**—*Are you fed up with the results of procrastinating?*

Make your dreams exhilarating and your goals motivating. Choose a dream that gets you totally fired up—then go for it! You can do it. Others have and you can too.

2 The *ORGANIZING* Section

➤ *Be specific about the items you list.* Give thoughtful consideration to the three major objectives you would like to accomplish each week. Complete this section on Sunday evening for the coming week, and be specific.

Here are three examples—weight loss, business productivity, and family encouragement. They will serve as a guide as you complete the *ORGANIZING* section for your own goals...

ORGANIZING Example #1
Weight Loss

GOAL—*Weigh 160 Pounds*
➤ **During the first few weeks, your list may look like this:**
1. Talk to my best friend and ask how they stay healthy and in shape.
2. Talk to my doctor about what I want to accomplish.
3. Begin walking briskly three times a week for 20 minutes.
4. Eat only fresh fruit in the morning.

➤ **Later weeks might look like this:**
1. Continue to follow my physician's recommendations, including limiting total calorie intake.
2. On Sunday, write a menu for every meal of the week.
3. Jog on Sunday. Take a brisk 30-minute walk on Monday, Wednesday, and Friday. Ride stationary bike for 30 minutes on Tuesday, Thursday, and Saturday.

ORGANIZING Example #2
Business Productivity

GOAL—*Increase Business by Ten Percent for the Month*
➤ **During the first few weeks, your list may look like this:**
1. Read at least one positive personal development book a month, i.e., 15 to 20 minutes a day.

2. Listen to motivational tapes when: I'm getting ready for work or bed, driving to work in the morning, taking my walk at lunch, returning home in the evening, and when I'm in the car traveling anywhere else.

3. Organize my telephone calls to prospects and customers the day before, so I'm ready to make the phone calls by the next day.

4. Attend continuing education opportunities—seminars and other related events to stay informed and motivated.

> **Later weeks might look like this:**

1. Having made an average of 23 phone calls a day last month (115 a week), increase that number by 20 percent. This week, make 138 calls.

2. Send a personal note to all of my new customers and associates of the last 90 days. I then follow up with a call to share new products and services, seek reorders, and ask for referrals.

3. Continuously strive for the next level of achievement by counseling with my leader or mentor monthly, and following their recommendations.

ORGANIZING Example #3
Family Encouragement

GOAL—Become a Better Spouse

> **During the first few weeks, your list may look like this:**

1. Plan a "date" with my spouse.

2. Listen to my spouse intently when they're talking to me—taking a sincere interest in what they're sharing by asking questions and supporting them.

3. Write my spouse an encouraging note.

> **Later weeks might look like this:**

1. Start an Appreciation/Admiration Board on the refrigerator listing one item, every day, that I appreciate or admire about my spouse.

2. Tape a love note onto their car steering wheel before my spouse leaves for work.

3. Plan a special night out for Saturday.

The purpose for your list under *ORGANIZING* is either to help you...

➤ Move methodically toward a new goal (Example #1).
➤ Increase your current performance level (Example #2).

or

➤ Achieve and maintain a consistent high level of caring effort (Example #3).

3   The *ACTING* Section

➤ *EVERY DAY, write down specifically what you did in pursuit of your goal.* Each action you take toward achieving your goal is important and you need to record it. After you write down a specific action, also record the amount of time it took you to complete it. (This tells you how much time you're investing in your goal.) For example, it may have taken you 15 minutes to plan your schedule for the week.

➤ *If you took no action on a particular day, write down "no action taken," forget about it and recommit to your goal. Go ahead and plan what you'll do the next day!* Do your best. No matter how much you plan to, you might not be able to take action on your goal every day due to circumstances beyond your control. The important thing is to get back on track. The objective of the *ACTING* section is to get you thinking about your goal every day and doing something toward its achievement in line with your other priorities. *Every single day* write down something in the *ACTING* section. This will help you stay focused on what you really want to accomplish and deal with distractions and any tendency to procrastinate.

➤ *If your nightly analysis reveals several days where you've taken no action on your goals, let your frustration drive you, not defeat you!* Today is past, but tomorrow is a new beginning. Let the pursuit of your goal begin again—with resolute determination! As you do this, day in and day out, you'll be surprised at home much progress you can make.

➤ *Don't fool yourself.* The point of *ACTING* is to help you move toward your goal. Actions that sabotage your success and keep you marching in place won't get you anywhere. For example, you may have found you need to do some research. But don't devote more time to it than necessary. If you have enough information to move ahead, then *stop looking* into it and *start getting* into it—and make it happen!

Here's an example of how of how an *ACTING* week's activities could look.

GOAL—*BUILDING MY OWN BUSINESS*

ACTING

What action did I take toward my dream today?						
Monday	Tuesday	Wednesday	Thursday	Friday	Saturday	Sunday
Wrote down 20 reasons why I want my own business	Thought about conversation with Julie	Shared my business plan with Chris	Called Chris about how to get started	No action taken	Went to a seminar and bought 3 books on personal growth	No action taken
15 minutes	10 minutes	2 hours	10 minutes	0	6 hours	0
Talked to Julie						
20 minutes						
Total: 35 minutes	Total: 10 minutes	Total 2 hours	Total: 10 minutes	Total: 0	Total: 6 hours	Total: 0

 The *REJECTING* Section

> *What did you allow to stop you from moving ahead on your goal today?* If you let something interfere with your working on your goal—discover why by asking yourself questions like these...

- *Was it my attitude?*
- *Was it a rejection letter?*
- *Was it a boss who said no?*
- *Was it discovering there's another step necessary?*
- *Did I fail to follow through?*
- *Did I do a poor job of managing my activities?*
- *Did I have a peak-performance mind-set?*
- *Would it have been better if I had included other people?*
- *Did I go through the proper channels?*
- *Was I unprepared?*
- *Did I get off track because of my action or inaction?*
- *Was my self-discipline weak?*
- *Did I negatively affect someone else?*
- *Was my energy and enthusiasm low?*
- *Did I take the "easy road" rather than do things correctly?*
- *Was my plan well thought out?*

> *Look at failures as positives.* As you tackle your goal objectives each day, don't be discouraged by failures or roadblocks. If they come, accept overcoming them as part of the process. They can teach you something valuable—what *not* to do. So, learn from them. Revise your plan of action if you need to, but keep on moving *forward!* Develop a mind-set that becomes more determined with each no. Remember, the more noes you get, the closer you are to a yes.

> *Don't repeat your mistakes.* Identify obstacles so you can develop a strategy for overcoming them. *The SOAR Per-*

formance Journal is only of value when you pay attention to what it tells you. *Invest time to learn from any unsuccessful efforts. Continually put yourself back on track to your goals, rejecting what doesn't work.*

Here's an example of how a *REJECTING* week's activities could look:

REJECTING

Did I allow anything to stop me today? If so, what?						
Monday	Tuesday	Wednesday	Thursday	Friday	Saturday	Sunday
OK	Lack of energy... I was too tired to really do much	OK	OK	Too much going on.	OK	Day to relax
What am I going to do to REJECT this obstacle?						
	Eat a lighter lunch.			Schedule activities better. Make goal a priority.		Nothing. Day of rest.

Your *SOAR* Performance Journal

When we live with purpose, we develop passion. And when we live with passion, we have the power to make incredible things happen in our lives!

This and the following page contain blank boxes for you to fill in and keep your own *SOAR* Performance Journal. You may want to copy these two pages, as you can use them over and over again.

What dream do I want to live? What am I passionate about accomplishing?
MY DREAM:_____

I am motivated to live this dream because _____

_____

When I live this dream, I will feel _____

_____

If I don't live this dream, I will feel _____

_____

MY LIFE PURPOSE: _____

What steps do I need to take this week to move closer to living my dream?

1. _____

2. _____

3. _____

ACTING

What actions did I take toward my dream today?						
Monday	Tuesday	Wednesday	Thursday	Friday	Saturday	Sunday

REJECTING

Did I allow anything to stop me today? If so, what?						
Monday	Tuesday	Wednesday	Thursday	Friday	Saturday	Sunday
What am I going to do to REJECT this obstacle?						

ABOUT THE AUTHOR

Shawn Anderson is a firm believer in the power of the human spirit. At 35, he had made it his mission to empower 1,000,000 people to lead a life of purpose and passionate existence. He is a powerful dreamer who is invigorated by the thought of helping others succeed and achieve their dreams. He finds nothing more exciting in life than helping others maximize their purpose . . . and win.

As a self-employed business developer, Shawn has proven his resourcefulness in building successful organizations, developing national events, and leading corporate fundraising activities. He is a motivator of people, a solidifier of ideas, and a magnifier of projects. He has a track record of taking ideas and dreams and then turning them into reality.

As an author and people builder, Shawn has written one other book: *Countdown to College: Preparing Your Student for Success in the Collegiate Universe*. Additionally, Shawn has written a weekly motivational/personal development column and is a professional public speaker.

He lives in Los Angeles, California.